Books for Sammies

Books for Sammies

THE AMERICAN LIBRARY ASSOCIATION AND WORLD WAR I

ARTHUR P. YOUNG

BETA PHI MU
1981

Beta Phi Mu Chapbook Number Fifteen
Published by Beta Phi Mu, Pittsburgh, Pennsylvania
ISBN 0-910230-15-3

Beta Phi Mu Publications Committee
Edward G. Holley
David Kaser
Harold Lancour
Wayne A. Wiegand, Chair

Library of Congress Cataloging Information follows:

Library of Congress Cataloging in Publication Data

Young, Arthur P.
  Books for Sammies.

  (Beta Phi Mu chapbook; no. 15)
  Revision of thesis (Ph. D.)—University of
Illinois at Urban-Champaign.
  ''Books and pamphlets banned by the War
Department'': p. 109
  Bibliography: p. 115
  Includes index.
  1. World War, 1914-1918—Libraries (in camps, etc.) 2.
American Library Association—History. I. Title. II. Series.
Z675.W2Y68 1981   027.6'6   81-17085
ISBN 0-910230-15-3   AACR2

Dedicated to
Patricia, John, Christopher
and
my parents

FOREWORD

Books for Sammies represents the fifteenth in a series of Beta Phi Mu chapbooks which began publication in 1953. The Society desires that each volume make a contribution to the literature of books and libraries and advance the art of book design. While the subjects of previously published chapbooks have covered such varied topics as bibliography, fine binding, unique manuscripts, and book design, the most persistent area of analysis continues to be library history. By selecting Dr. Young's manuscript for publication, Beta Phi Mu adds another significant volume on library history to its chapbooks list.

Arthur Young is eminently qualified to write a history of the American Library Association during World War I. His undergraduate and graduate years at Tufts University and the University of Massachusetts concentrated heavily upon the study of American history. He took a library science degree at Syracuse University in 1969, and completed his dissertation at the Graduate School of Library Science at the University of Illinois in 1976. This chapbook represents a revised version of that dissertation. Dr. Young has also served as Head of Reader Services and Social Science Bibliographer at the State University of New York at Cortland, and is currently Assistant Dean for Public Services and Associate Professor at the University of Alabama Library. In addition to numerous reviews, Dr. Young has published a score of articles on library history and academic library service. He is currently serving on the Editorial Board of the *Journal of Library History*.

Books for Sammies is the definitive study of the American Library Association's activities during World War I. We offer it to our readers as a scholarly contribution to library literature.

W.A.W.

PREFACE

Several weeks after the United States entered World War I in April 1917, the American Library Association (ALA) began preparations for the worldwide distribution of library materials to American soldiers. The Executive Board of the Association appointed a permanent War Service Committee in June 1917 to oversee what became known as the Library War Service. No one could foresee in 1917 that the Library War Service program would remain active long after the Armistice and the protracted demobilization. By 1920, the Association had mounted two financial campaigns and raised over $5,000,000 from public donations, secured Carnegie Corporation funds for the erection of thirty-six camp library buildings, distributed approximately 10,000,000 books and magazines, and provided library collections to nearly 5,000 locations. Just over 1,100 library workers served in libraries sponsored by the Association. Although the War Service Committee was discharged in the summer of 1920, a number of war-related activities continued well into the postwar decade. *

The Library War Service represented the ALA's most ambitious attempt to cooperate with other welfare agencies. Experimental forms of library service, such as books-by-mail and braille texts, were used extensively. Recurring themes in the history of librarianship, including censorship, the status of women, and elitism appeared again during the war. A new generation of library leaders, which included Carl H. Milam, Malcolm G. Wyer, and Joseph L. Wheeler, were prominent participants in the Library War Service. Finally, the Association's war work produced a number of tangible legacies: formation of the American Library in Paris; establishment of the American Merchant Marine Library Association; greater concern with international library development; and assimilation of the wartime library programs by the military departments and other government agencies.

Operating under constraints of limited funds, a small membership (about 3,300 in 1917), and external supervision, the American Library Association's Library War Service program may be judged an unusually successful venture. Competent leadership was undeniably important; but even more decisive was the consensus among library leaders regarding the administration and operation of the camp library sys-

---

* Throughout this study, the terms Library War Service, Association, and ALA are used interchangeably except when a clear distinction is warranted.

tem. Four management-related concepts and functions—bureaucratization, standardization, cooperation, and publicity—represented the significant points of consensus.

Bureaucratization may be characterized as an evolutionary process exemplified by the consolidation of decision-making power, the formulation of rules of conduct, the institution of hierarchical relationships, and the division of labor. The centralization of policy-making authority, the specialization of functions, and the application of technical (professional) competence were essential features of the Library War Service. A correlative of the bureaucratic organization, standardization is an important factor relating to operational efficiency. Uniform procedures for the selection and shipment of library materials, and the construction of camp library buildings were notable examples. Cooperation, or the nature and extent of organizational interdependence between the ALA and other agencies, was a particularly important attribute of the Library War Service. The Library War Service was not an autonomous program; the Association was often dependent upon the federal government and various civilian social service organizations. The indispensability, as well as vicissitudes, of these contacts is a central focus of this study. Lastly, the unprecedented use of mass publicity by the ALA during and after the war played a pivotal role in book collection drives and fund raising campaigns.

Additional topics are reviewed in terms of library traditions and the contemporary social context. For example, did such issues as censorship, job opportunities for female librarians, and service to immigrants generally confirm or deviate from past professional patterns? And did the ALA's wartime practices regarding these issues differ from the national experience? The extent to which the ALA's wartime activities influenced postwar library developments in the areas of adult education, military library service, and international librarianship are examined. Because the wartime program extended the Association's traditional constituency and generated expectations for a national program of library revitalization, the postwar episode known as the "Enlarged Program" is also briefly treated.

This study is a revision of the author's doctoral dissertation, which was completed at the Graduate School of Library Science, University of Illinois. It is a pleasure to acknowledge the many debts incurred. Professor Donald W. Krummel guided the study with wise counsel and infinite patience. His suggestions, stylistic and substantive, were enormously helpful. Professor Lucille M. Wert contributed numerous, constructive comments. Dr. Herbert Goldhor, director of the Graduate School of Library Science, was supportive throughout and generously provided financial assistance. I am also indebted to the Graduate School, University of Illinois, for a dissertation research grant.

I am especially grateful to the knowledgeable archival staff of the University of Illinois Library: Maynard J. Brichford, archivist; Charles B. Elston, former assistant archivist, now at Marquette University; and Mrs. Evelyn H. Arvedson, technical assistant. Mr. Brichford, particularly, rendered thoughtful assistance and suggested a number of fruitful investigative leads. Ida F. Wilson at the Library of Congress and Timothy Nenninger at the National Archives were unfailingly responsive to my requests. Florence Anderson, former secretary of the Carnegie Corporation of New York, provided me with pertinent Corporation minutes. With the customary absolution for my errors of fact or interpretation, appreciation is extended to the following scholars for their critiques and words of encouragement: Dee Garrison, Rutgers University; Edward G. Holley, University of North Carolina; and Michael Harris and Wayne Wiegand, University of Kentucky. The manuscript was typed, with skill and forebearance, by Mrs. Margaret Tilton and Ms. Sondra Annice Tucker.

Arthur P. Young
Amelia Gayle Gorgas Library
University of Alabama

ILLUSTRATIONS

CONTENTS

ONE

Organizing for Library War Service

When the "guns of August" shattered the fragile European balance of power in 1914, most Americans confidently expected that the United States would not be drawn into the conflict. On August 4, 1914, President Wilson issued an official proclamation of neutrality, but for the next three years he found it increasingly difficult to pursue a policy of impartiality toward the belligerents. In fact, America's drift toward war was accelerated by many causes over which Wilson had little control: the Anglo-French sympathy of many Americans; the systematic propaganda campaign of the Allies; Germany's use of unrestricted submarine warfare; and interception of the Zimmermann telegram, revealing a German plot to involve Mexico in a war against the United States. Those events and attitudes explain some of the objective reasons for American intervention, but a deeper understanding requires an analysis of President Wilson's perception of world affairs and ideological predispositions. Ultimately, the majority of Americans entered and fought the war, and based their postwar expectations on the views of their president.[1]

Wilson's liberalism was a subtle blend of progressivism, anti-imperialism, commercial expansionism, and moral idealism. As a nationalist, the president often stressed the importance of American capitalism to a stable world order. Although opposed to exploitative imperialism, Wilson saw American economic strength as a key element in restructuring a peaceful world based upon mediation and rational discourse. Through America's moral and economic supremacy, and with the help of other civilized powers, the world could achieve peace and live under international law. The German submarine threat was an obvious challenge to Wilson's vision of liberal internationalism, but a more emo-

1

tive ideological rationale was needed to justify intervention. With the resumption of unrestricted submarine warfare and the March revolution in Russia, the president and his advisers finally conceded the inevitability of war as a conflict between German autocracy and American democracy.[2]

Many American citizens and soldiers were inspired by the president's moral certitude during the war. The war narratives of soldiers are replete with references to the Great War (an exuberant designation) as a chivalric quest to rescue humanity and to preserve democracy. Waging the war to make the world "safe for democracy" appealed to America's sense of moral justice, but without a strong element of national self-interest the commitment could not be sustained.[3] Heavy sacrifices on the battlefield and defeat of the League of Nations contributed to self-doubts over the war's purpose and to massive postwar disillusionment.

The advent of war led to the increased use of propaganda, the dilution of civil liberties, and scattered opposition to government policies. Divided sentiment over the war prompted creation of the Committee on Public Information, a government agency designed to mobilize public opinion behind the war effort. George Creel, the committee's chairman, was a progressive Denver journalist who brought exceptional organizational talent to his assignment. He instituted a voluntary press censorship which worked remarkably well. By war's end, Creel had dispatched over 75,000 lecturers and published ninety-four items (75,000,000 copies) concerning American war aims. Creel's propaganda literature often portrayed Germany as the Hun aggressor, devoid of moral scruples.[4]

Volunteer patriotic organizations proliferated and their zealotry sometimes approached vigilantism. The American Protective League, which was sponsored by the Department of Justice, often acted illegally in its campaigns to root out disloyalty. Ugly anti-Germanism was rampant; sauerkraut was renamed "liberty cabbage;" schools and churches dropped the German language; and the loyalty of many German-Americans was impugned. Other groups, notably socialists and pacifists, were also harassed and not infrequently jailed. The Creel committee, and the volunteer groups particularly, contributed to nationalistic excesses during the war and to a new wave of postwar emotionalism (anti-Bolshevism) culminating in the Red Scare of 1919-1920.[5]

Fear of internal dissension and treason activated a series of congressional acts which curtailed civil liberties. The Espionage Act of June

15, 1917 empowered the postmaster general to withhold seditious materials from the mails. Postmaster General Albert S. Burleson used his powers indiscriminately and with little overt opposition from President Wilson. Newspapers and magazines withheld from the mails included *The Masses,* a radical anti-war sheet; Victor Berger's *Milwaukee Leader,* a Socialist party organ; and the *Nation.* A number of books were seized by postal authorities, among them Hugo Freytag-Loringhoven's *Deductions from the World War.* Succumbing to informal pressure, publishers also withdrew titles, as in the case of the National Security League's complaint against Ellen Key's *War, Peace, and the Future.* By the spring of 1918, the War Department caught the censorship fever and banned scores of books from camp libraries.[6]

With civil liberties under siege and a nation at war, it was inevitable that reformism would lose some of its momentum. World War I did not eclipse progressivism entirely, but despair, frustration, and indirection were prevalent. Although the war sidetracked reform, especially for blacks and immigrants, some progressive causes made headway. Prohibition and the women's suffrage movement were perhaps the two most conspicuous issues which not only survived the war but achieved legislative protection soon afterward. Several reform ideas found expression in the social welfare programs of the War Department's Commission on Training Camp Activities. Consisting of seven welfare organizations, including the ALA and the Young Men's Christian Association (YMCA), the commission applied the techniques of social work, recreation, and community organization to the tasks of entertaining and protecting American troops. Foremost among the social crusades espoused by the commission were social hygiene (principally the fight against prostitution) and prohibition.[7]

Creation of the Commission on Training Camp Activities and the many governmental agencies which monitored the nation's resources accentuated a number of trends which may be subsumed under the concept of modernization. Modernization, or the development of organizational society in America, was a complex phenomenon distinguished by a continuing extension of control over and manipulation of the external environment. Three facets of modernization, each with roots in the nineteenth century, became more explicit during and after the war: bureaucratization (centralization, specialization, systemization); professionalization (educational standards, expertise, client service, autonomy); and government/private sector interdependence. The convergence of these historical processes was occasionally traumatic for librarians. For example, although librarians were bureaucratically inclined practitioners, they were also members of a nascent profession. Consequently, tensions occasionally surfaced during the war when the bureaucratic impulse toward centralization and control collided with the profession's sense of autonomy and independent judgment.[8]

Within this ambivalent setting—one suffused with moralistic overtones, subdued progressivism, emerging professionalism, and government-induced conformity—librarians and their national organization responded to the Great War.

Recalling a hasty return from the Leipzig Book Exhibit in the summer of 1914, Mary E. Ahern, editor of *Public Libraries,* expressed disappointment over disruption of the fair and concern for librarians here and abroad who "shared in the consequent sorrow" of the European war. Ahern's reaction to the commencement of hostilities mirrored the initial sentiments of many librarians, a mixture of disbelief, muted anger, and noninvolvement.[9] Editorially, *Library Journal* expressed a dazed reaction:

> [The war] raises no feelings with us but horrified bewilderment, for our own professional friendships are as sincere north of the Rhine as south of it. The world will always be the debtor of German thoroughness in scientific research as it is the debtor of French brilliancy in analysis and English sanity in things political. Our sympathy is with each and all of the contestants, our only hope an early return to peace.[10]

International professional sympathy continued throughout the war, but a decided pro-Ally bias became increasingly evident during the period of neutrality (1914-1917). After American intervention, most librarians combined their strong support of Allied goals with an unmistakable animus against Germany and literature supporting the German cause. Castigating Germany as the enemy of education and the ideals of civilization, a Boston librarian-columnist asked his readers in October 1918 to "stop worrying about the ship-load of Boche literature on the dock at Amsterdam. If it gets blown up—who cares?"[11]

Several factors help to explain why librarians supported the war so intensely. As social agencies, libraries have historically reflected contemporary values, and World War I was no exception. For many Americans the Great War became a morally charged, even spiritualized struggle, and librarians readily absorbed the symbolism and patriotic emotionalism. The sacrificial ideal and the heritage of the library as a moral arbiter of reading tastes were strong undercurrents in the library profession. And these attributes blended easily with the wartime

4

emphasis on national solidarity and altruistic service. Allied propaganda before America's entry, government surveillance of the media during the war, and the cultural affinity of America with England and France also contributed to the pro-Ally stance of librarians. Along with embracing the national war spirit, librarians were exhilarated by the prospects for spreading the gospel of the library's value to society. [12]

Librarians were generally reticent about expressing their views in print prior to the American declaration. Those who did publish their views claimed impartiality toward the warring parties—a sincere but inaccurate assertion. Invoking the library as the citadel of "free inquiry" and "complete enlightenment," George Bowerman of the Washington, D.C. Public Library asked librarians in 1915 to stock and circulate peace literature. Bowerman cautioned librarians to differentiate their private convictions from their official responsibilities. Literature on the peace movement should be promoted because of the library's "essential character" and as a matter of "self-preservation." [13] In 1915, Bowerman's liberal views were not typical; after 1917, similar comments would find a generally hostile audience among librarians.

After America had declared war and the ALA had announced its program of service, librarians responded enthusiastically and mobilized the library press to enlist support from the profession. Articles and editorials exhorted librarians to meet the "test" and "challenge" of the war. Many writers stressed the need for involvement because the nation was fighting for the preservation of democracy and Western civilization. [14] Another theme stressed the need for citizens and soldiers to understand the ideals of their country and the library's key role in fulfilling that goal. [15] Winning over the foreign born, who were seen as a "very real danger" to social stability, was also advanced as a desirable objective. [16]

Jessie Welles of the Wisconsin Free Library Commission tersely summarized the library's paternalistic mission: "Great masses of the people do not understand their duty nor their country's need. Organize your unit to serve by informing and inspiring every citizen." [17] The positive call to service was often supplemented by a threat to librarians not promoting the war effort. A widely quoted Wisconsin editorial, entitled "Is Your Library a Slacker?," left no doubt about the fate of uncooperative public librarians: ". . . to be neutral now is to be disloyal." [18]

Cooperation with outside agencies and groups was a prominent feature of many library programs. Literature from the Committee on Public Information and Herbert Hoover's United States Food Administration was channeled to thousands of libraries. Edith Guerrier of the

Boston Public Library was chief of the Library Bureau in the Food Administration. In this capacity she instituted a newsletter, *Food News for Libraries,* and travelled extensively to educate librarians about the need for food conservation materials and exhibits. Dozens of welfare and patriotic organizations held meetings in libraries, and various local liberty loan campaigns were launched in a library setting. Immigrants were encouraged to become "Americanized" through library reading programs, and children's story hours became vehicles for inculcating patriotism.[19]

Delimiting the boundaries of book selection in wartime was a difficult task for librarians. Contemporary discussions of censorship document librarians' cautious approach and discomfiture over the need to debate the issue at all. Ernest C. Richardson, librarian of Princeton University and respected for his intellectual grasp of library matters, considered censorship an inherent responsibility of a free society. Free speech and a free press were "subject to the principle of non-interference with the freedom of others" as evidenced by libel and slander laws. Since libraries normally excluded books of an immoral character and those defaming religions, Richardson argued that seditious literature should be collected by large libraries for future research, but withheld from general circulation during the war.[20] Most librarians interpreted their selection and service responsibilities as articulated by Richardson, but there were courageous exceptions. John Cotton Dana, curmudgeonly director of the Newark Free Public Library, refused to withdraw eight books sympathetic to Germany when pressured by a group of local censors.[21]

Librarians' rhetoric about their impartiality during neutrality was belied by their acquisition and circulation practices. Gift books favorable to the Allies poured into American libraries from Wellington House, England's secret propaganda agency. Claiming a print run of 200,000 copies for some titles, Wellington House sent the books as gifts from British and Scottish professors, never disclosing their true source. In a comprehensive study of library holdings of propaganda literature, Ralph Esterquest analyzed nine public library collections to determine the pattern of gift books received during 1914-1917. The average library received 50 to 100 titles, with a better than 50 to 1 ratio of pro-Ally to pro-German items. A check of 227 Wellington House titles against the University of Illinois catalog revealed that 206 titles, or 92 percent, were held. Comparison of a list of pro-German titles, compiled during a U.S. Senate propaganda investigation, against the Illinois catalog corroborated the relatively low level of holdings favorable to the Central Powers. Only 30 of the 55 titles, or 55 percent, were available.[22]

Esterquest also traced 123 propaganda titles cited in Harold D. Lasswell's *Propaganda Technique in the World War* to ascertain if they were found in the collections of ten public libraries (including those of Boston, Chicago, and Los Angeles). The titles, issued during 1914-1918, were classified as favoring the Allies (56), Germans (57), and advocating neutrality (10). The average public library held 47 percent of the Allied propaganda titles and only 9 percent of the pro-German items.[23] Most American librarians favored the Allied cause, and it is reasonable to assume that some compromised the profession's generally avowed goal of providing equitable treatment to all points of view on contemporary public issues.

Those academic libraries that did want to acquire German and Austrian publications for scholarly use and preservation were plagued by importation difficulties. To alleviate this problem, the ALA appointed a Committee on Importation chaired by Frank P. Hill of the Brooklyn Public Library in November 1916. Hill and the committee's able secretary, McKendree L. Raney of the Johns Hopkins University Library, were soon engaged in an international diplomatic offensive to find a solution. Working through the Department of State, the committee persuaded the British Foreign Office in the summer of 1917 to negotiate the release of a shipment detained for a year at Rotterdam. By January 1918, the Association obtained a trade permit from the Department of State which regularized the importation of library materials. The committee acted as an intermediary for university libraries, securing enemy publications from Berne, London, Rotterdam, and other cities.[24]

Concurrent with the response of individual libraries and librarians to the war, the American Library Association became involved to a degree unexpected by anyone in April 1917. That involvement did not seem foreordained by the Association's past record.

Between its founding in 1876 and 1917, the Association maintained a strong public library orientation and drew most of its membership from New England and the Midwest. Its conferences, often held in resort settings, stressed fellowship, speeches, and discussions; and were memorable for their frequent social outings. Few ALA presidents charted new courses for the organization; most were content with reflecting on the Association's past accomplishments. Much energy was expended by ALA leaders on defining the library profession, devising new methods for making libraries more efficient, debating the merits of popular literature, and convincing the public of the library's educational value. Major commitments to serve the handicapped, the foreign born, and children did not occur until the early

War Service Committee (1918) (l-r): Thomas L. Montgomery (president, ALA), Gratia Countryman, Frank P. Hill, James I. Wyer, Matthew S. Dudgeon, Electra C. Doren, Richard R. Bowker, Arthur E. Bostwick

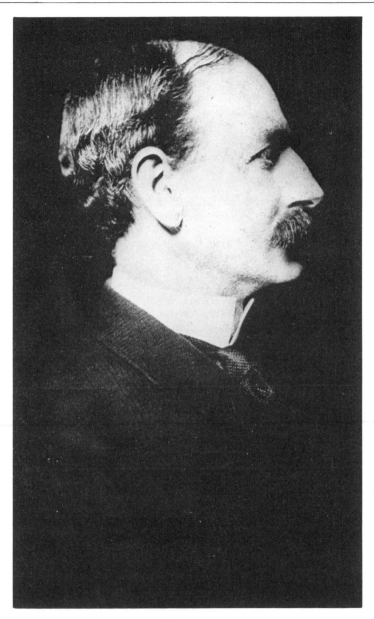

Herbert Putnam

years of the twentieth century. The Association's first four decades represented a period of professional introspection and organizational consolidation, with little impact on external agencies.[25]

By 1917, the Association did not seem strong enough, either in terms of resources or professional maturity, to assume the task of supplying reading matter to an American army of several million men. Membership in the Association had reached 3,346, and the ALA conducted its affairs with an annual budget of just over $24,000. Burton E. Stevenson, librarian-novelist and future leader in the Association's overseas program, penned this unflattering portrait of the ALA on the eve of its wartime service:

> The American Library Association was merely a humdrum professional organization, wrapped round with tradition, settled in its habits of thought, and chiefly occupied with matters of technical detail. Its members were quiet, inoffensive, well-behaved people, cherishing the same hobby and agreeing upon everything except whether a large circulation was a merit or a disgrace.[26]

The opportunity to change this image would begin a few weeks after America's declaration of war against Germany.

In April 1917 Herbert Putnam, Librarian of Congress, and Frederick P. Keppel, future Third Assistant Secretary of War, met for breakfast at Washington's elegant Cosmos Club. Putnam broached the subject of furnishing books to the American army. Convinced that Putnam's suggestion merited further consideration, Keppel arranged for Putnam to see Secretary of War Newton D. Baker the following morning. As Keppel recalled the incident, "these two readers and scholars kept a room full of senators and diplomats and other dignitaries waiting while they laid the plans for that wartime service which gave the American Library Association its chance to show what it could do."[27] Although this account of Putnam's meeting with Secretary Baker makes it clear that ALA provided the initiative in offering its services, it fails to convey the confusion surrounding development of the Association's program which prevailed from April to the annual conference in June.

The ALA Executive Board established a Committee on Mobilization and War Service Plans in April 1917. Herbert Putnam, who was appointed chairman of the committee on April 30, served with six other distinguished members of the library community: Arthur E. Bostwick, director of the St. Louis Public Library; Richard R. Bowker, library publisher; Gratia A. Countryman, director of the Minneapolis Public Library; Matthew S. Dudgeon, executive secretary of the Wisconsin Free Library Commission; Alice S. Tyler, director of the Western Reserve University Library School; and James I. Wyer, Jr., director of the New York State Library. To this preliminary committee fell the task of sorting out recommendations from the membership and formulating a program for review at the annual conference.[28]

James Wyer perceived a distinct, though not fully independent role for the ALA, which was later incorporated into the committee's report. Wyer believed that the Association might coordinate library service through YMCA facilities, but that the ALA should retain control over book selection and preparation, and furnish trained personnel to administer libraries. Alice Tyler suggested that state library agencies should coordinate a travelling library system for soldiers. Phineas L. Windsor, director of the University of Illinois Library, urged the consideration of a number of topics: identifying the effects of war on reading and library finances; creating local historical collections on the war; and defining the relationship between the ALA and the YMCA.[29]

In early May, Putnam advised the YMCA that the ALA ought to play a supportive role in a library program administered by that organization. Putnam went on to observe that many books would need to be purchased and that explicit criteria must be developed for gift items.[30] By late May Putnam was less enthusiastic about the YMCA. He contacted Raymond B. Fosdick of the newly formed Commission on Training Camp Activities to suggest that a service "more authoritative" than the YMCA could be performed by the commission. Further, the Library of Congress could transfer its duplicate books to a federal agency more easily than to a private group.[31] Fosdick responded that the commission would oversee library service, but that the YMCA was the prime candidate to administer the program.[32] Putnam, upset over a report that the Red Cross was also planning to distribute books, confided to Frank P. Hill that "thus far there is duplication and confusion."[33]

On June 22, at the ALA's annual conference in Louisville, Putnam presented the Committee on Mobilization's report to the Association. Early in the report, he cited several precedents of library service for soldiers: German military travelling libraries; state library work with local camps in the United States; the YMCA Mexican border service; and British programs for soldiers and prisoners of war.[34] After reviewing these precedents, and consulting with various agencies, committee members concluded that an ALA library operation on a "vast scale" was desirable. Furnishing reading materials to the soldier would relieve his "depressing tedium" and "dangerous temptation." For the

11

American Library Association, the present moment "seems an extraordinary opportunity" which would "add notably to the prestige of the Association." Whether or not to act independently was the key issue, and on this point the committee was circumspect.[35]

Cognizant of the plans of other welfare societies and the Commission on Training Camp Activities, the Mobilization Committee recommended close cooperation with those bodies in order to prevent duplication. Two forms of aid which the Association should offer, regardless of which organization administered the program, were the preparation of book lists and the recruitment of trained librarians to manage camp collections. If the ALA wished to consider independent action, funds would be required for books, camp buildings, and transportation. Separate operations in Europe were not recommended as feasible. After outlining the alternatives, the Mobilization Committee cautiously decided to recommend the appointment of a permanent War Service Committee and to spend the summer formulating more detailed plans.[36]

After Putnam presented the report, Bostwick read a paper by Theodore W. Koch, Chief of the Library of Congress' Order Division, on the British war library service. Books and magazines were furnished to British troops, starting in late 1914, through four agencies: the British Red Cross and Order of St. John War Library; the Camps Library; the YMCA; and the British Prisoners of War Book Scheme (Educational). The War Library provided reading matter for war casualities in over 2,100 hospitals in Great Britain and Europe. Several million books were donated by the public and some of these were sold to enable the purchase of more desirable items. The Camps Library performed a similar service for colonial troops serving throughout the United Kingdom and for British troops fighting in Europe. Reports from the soldiers using all of these services indicated that recreational and educational materials were needed and appreciated.[37]

The YMCA was represented at the ALA conference by William Orr, educational secretary of the YMCA's National War Work Council. Anxious to cooperate with the ALA, Orr outlined his organization's educational and recreational plans for the new American army. Camp libraries were contemplated as part of the YMCA educational program, but the details were still vague. When asked if ALA books would be segregated from YMCA books, or if ALA librarians should be placed under YMCA jurisdiction or retain a separate identity, Orr declined to commit his organization. He asked for more time and controlled experimentation before making these decisions.[38]

At the end of the conference President Brown appointed a permanent War Service Committee to be headed by James I. Wyer. Continued from the preliminary committee were Bostwick, Countryman, Dudgeon, and Tyler. Two new members, Edwin H. Anderson of the New York Public Library, and Frank P. Hill were added. Of the two men not continuing on the permanent committee, Bowker would become a committee member in 1918 and Putnam would assume directorship of the committee's administrative arm, the Library War Service. As expected, the committee was composed of veteran professionals and weighted heavily in favor of public libraries and state library agencies.

The committee's composition was reasonably stable during the war: Tyler was unable to serve and was replaced by Electra C. Doren of the Dayton (Ohio) Public Library. Bostwick and Dudgeon resigned in the fall of 1917 and were succeeded by William H. Brett of the Cleveland Public Library and Charles F. D. Belden of the Boston Public Library. Bowker took Brett's place when the latter died in a tragic automobile accident in August 1918. Mary L. Titcomb of the Washington County (Maryland) Free Library replaced Gratia Countryman, who resigned in late 1919. Wyer, Anderson, Hill, and Doren, by remaining on the committee from 1917 to 1920, provided essential continuity.

After being apprised of the ALA's war service resolutions at the Louisville conference, the Commission on Training Camp Activities invited the Association through Herbert Putnam to assume responsibility for library service in the thirty-two camps.[39] Fosdick proposed a central library in each camp under ALA control, to be erected from private funds which the ALA would have to secure. The YMCA would act as a distributing agent in other camp locations and the commission would pay for the ALA's heating and lighting costs. Perhaps as a concession to professional pride, the War Service Committee and library periodicals portrayed the library program as originating with the commission's unsolicited request to the ALA. The evidence contradicts these reports. It was Putnam who asked Fosdick on June 27 to invite the ALA to undertake library service for the commission.[40]

The Commission on Training Camp Activities, created in April 1917, provided various kinds of recreational and educational services for the American soldier in the United States and Europe. Secretary of War Newton D. Baker was particularly anxious not to allow the unnatural condition of war to subvert the moral climate and social stability of the new army:

These boys are going to France; they are going to face conditions that

13

we do not like to talk about, that we do not like to think about. They are going into a heroic enterprise and heroic enterprises involve sacrifices. I want them armed; I want them adequately armed and clothed by their government; but I want them to have invisible armor to take with them. I want them to have an armor made up of a set of social habits replacing those of their homes and communities, a set of social habits and a state of social mind born in the training camps, a new soldier state of mind, so that when they get overseas and are removed from the reach of our comforting and restraining and helpful hand, they will have gotten such a state of habits as will constitute a moral and intellectual armor for their protection overseas.[41]

The commission implemented Baker's ideas by setting up recreational and educational facilities in the camps, and by establishing a zone around each camp within which liquor and brothels were prohibited. At the end of 1917 Fosdick could proudly report to Baker that 110 red light districts had been closed, that the venereal disease rate had plummeted, and that drunkenness was no longer a serious problem.[42]

Together with the YMCA and the Playground and Recreation Association (organized in the war as the War Camp Community Service), the American Library Association was selected in the initial group of private agencies to affiliate with the commission. Because of the YMCA's refusal to conduct its work on a nonsectarian basis, Fosdick and Baker reluctantly permitted the Knights of Columbus and the Jewish Welfare Board to join the commission. With the addition of the Young Women's Christian Association and the Salvation Army, the commission would coordinate the activities of seven welfare societies. Although each group had separate responsibilities, the benefit of confederation was realized when the seven societies conducted a unified campaign for public funds in November 1918. Fosdick later regretted not placing the organizations under direct military control. The YMCA, for example, was besieged with complaints regarding administration of the canteen system in Europe.[43]

The American Library Association worked most closely with the YMCA and the War Camp Community Service. By far the largest organization affiliated with the commission, the YMCA furnished recreational, educational, and religious programs in nearly every military camp in the United States and Europe. Its educational offerings included classes in literacy, Americanization, vocational improvement, and art appreciation. Along with providing numerous outlets for ALA books, the YMCA purchased enormous quantities of educational books for its own programs.[44] The War Camp Community Service organized the resources of over 300 local communities near camps for soldiers on leave and was more hospitable to black soldiers than any other agency.[45] Hostess houses in the camps, where families and friends could meet with soldiers, were maintained by the Young Women's Christian Association.[46] Athletic equipment, food, and magazines were furnished by the Knights of Columbus in 461 locations across the United States.[47] One hundred sixty-five centers catering to the religious and personal needs of Jewish soldiers were operated by the Jewish Welfare Board.[48] The most highly praised of the welfare societies, the Salvation Army, fielded over 1,500 officers to run ambulance services, distribute food, and assist widows and orphans.[49]

Recognizing the need to get underway immediately, Wyer appointed subcommittees before the conference adjourned: Finance (Frank P. Hill), Publicity (Arthur E. Bostwick), Camp Libraries (Edwin H. Anderson), State Agencies (Matthew S. Dudgeon), Local Agencies (Gratia A. Countryman), Food Information (Claribel Barnett), Library War Manual (George F. Bowerman), Federal Publications (Herman H. B. Meyer), Transportation (Richard H. Johnston), Book Selection (Benjamin Adams), and Library War Week (Carl H. Milam). The Book Selection Committee went to work immediately and by September had produced a list of 5,000 titles recommended for camp libraries. Dudgeon quickly enlisted state library agencies to serve as liaisons with the War Service Committee. Milam's group was busy on the publicity front throughout the summer.[50]

Carl Milam, youthful (thirty-three years old) and aggressive director of the Birmingham (Alabama) Public Library, realized the need for national publicity and promptly produced the War Service Committee's first publication. A four-page tabloid bulletin, *War Service Library Week*, was issued on July 15, 1917 and distributed to the nation's libraries.[51] Libraries were urged to set aside a week in September or October to emphasize the value of libraries to the civilian population in their war efforts. Libraries were also requested to issue war-related book lists, to coordinate library programs with other community organizations, and to prepare publicity materials for later release. Events would overtake the idea of a Library War Week and it would never be held. But the gears were in motion and the initial publicity effort completed. In August 1917, the first number of the *War Library Bulletin* appeared. For the next two years, this slickly edited publication served as the major communication link between the War Service Committee, military camps, local libraries, and the nation's press.

In the middle of August, the ALA Executive Board instructed the War Service Committee to proceed with the task of providing books for the troops and to solicit funds in the Association's name. Two weeks later, George B. Utley, the ALA's executive secretary, became secretary of the War Service Committee, and Matthew Dudgeon was hired as director of camp libraries, the first salaried position in the Library War Service. Over the next two months, architectural plans for the camp libraries were approved and Frank Hill's finance committee conducted a successful campaign for $1.5 million. Financially solvent and committed to a major program of service, the War Service Committee was now ready to consolidate its activities under a new administrative arrangement.[52]

Meeting in Washington, D.C. on October 4, the committee conferred the title of general director on Herbert Putnam. Twice president of ALA (1898, 1903-1904) and near the zenith of his power as Librarian of Congress (1899-1939), Putnam would manage the Library War Service until December 13, 1919, when he was succeeded by Carl Milam. Few individuals are indispensable, but it is difficult to imagine another librarian who could have galvanized the Association's war program as Putnam did. Self-assured, meticulous, and urbane, Putnam was a formidable administrator and an equally good judge of character. He was able to identify and to attract to his staff many of the nation's most promising librarians who were at the threshold of distinguished careers.

Putnam's appointment was accompanied by a generous grant of administrative authority. James Wyer, Putnam's superior, remained chairman of the War Service Committee throughout the war and vigorously supported him. As general director, Putnam was empowered to define jobs, recruit personnel, set wages, negotiate contracts with outside agencies, and approve reading lists. Although the Library War Service budget required approval by the War Service Committee, Putnam set many of the fiscal priorities and enjoyed a great deal of latitude over expenditures.

Putnam moved decisively to unify and to centralize the Library War Service. Headquarters were transferred from their temporary location in the Washington, D.C. Public Library to the Library of Congress. On November 17 all of the subcommittees formed at the Louisville conference, excepting those on food and finance, were dissolved. Also in November, Carl Milam and Joseph L. Wheeler of the Youngstown (Ohio) Public Library were designated assistants to Putnam. Wheeler, who stayed until July 1918, managed camp library operations after Dudgeon left in December, while Milam became Putnam's senior lieutenant for two years. Many other prominent librarians served at the Library of Congress for brief periods on special assignments. Phineas L. Windsor assisted for several months on book selection, and Josephine Rathbone of the Pratt Institute (Brooklyn, New York) advised Putnam on personnel matters. The staff increased rapidly: from seventeen on January 1, 1918 to forty-six on June 20, 1918, and to eighty-three on February 1, 1919.[53]

An exhibit room in the Library of Congress' Maps and Charts Division served as the home of the Library War Service. Every phase of the war work was coordinated from this office. Cramped quarters, a hectic schedule, and long hours were endured by every member of the staff. Putnam never submitted any charge to the ALA for these accommodations and detailed many Library of Congress staff members to the war program at no expense. Demands of the Library War Service, and staff losses to the military service and other jobs, exacted a heavy toll on the Library of Congress. Between January 1, 1917 and June 30, 1918, Putnam lamented the staggering loss of 226 personnel out of a total force of 415.[54]

Once it was administratively defined, the Library War Service turned its attention to obtaining funds and books, constructing camp library buildings, and recruiting personnel.

TWO

Mobilizing Resources

The charge to provide library service for the armed forces became the Association's most compelling challenge. Organizing and managing the Library War service would lead the ALA into many new and unfamiliar activities. Since funds were not allocated for camp libraries by the federal government, the Association conducted two financial campaigns and sponsored three book collection drives. A grant from the Carnegie Corporation for camp library buildings enabled the Association to erect its own facilities and to make itself known on the military posts. As the program expanded, hundreds of librarians were recruited for service in the domestic camps and in Europe. Still other librarians became part of the administrative staff at the Library of Congress. A network of dispatch offices was created to facilitate the collection and distribution of library materials. Before any services could be activated, however, a major solicitation for funds would be required.

As early as the Louisville conference (June 1917), the War Service Committee realized that a substantial sum of money would be needed for even a modest library program. Before the conference had adjourned, a Dollar-a-Month fund was started to help underwrite a national campaign. In their appeal to Association members, Frank Hill and George Utley declared that "if we succeed in this emergency in rendering national service, libraries are going to be a national and community force as never before;" but should libraries fail, the two warned, they would be "looked on as weak, dreary, go-sit-in-the-corner affairs that are not worth public support."[1] Although a few pledges amounting to $100 per month had been collected by the end of the conference, funds to conduct a national drive were meager. Frank Hill, chairman of the War Finance Committee, initially scheduled the campaign for late summer and called for $628,700 to be solicited from ALA members, local libraries, and the general public.[2]

Following the commission's invitation to the ALA, and the decision to submit a proposal to the Carnegie Corporation in July for $320,000, the first-year target was raised to $1 million. In August, after meeting with Harold Braddock, an experienced fund raiser for the Red Cross, the Finance Committee concluded that $50,000 would be required to conduct the campaign. Principal underwriters, who were promised return of their money after the fund drive, included ALA; local libraries; Baker & Taylor, a library book supplier; and the Rockefeller Foundation, which contributed $25,000.[3]

Encouraged by the receipt of these funds, Library War Service leaders formulated definite plans. Representation on the War Finance Committee was enlarged, a Library War Council was created, and a campaign director and field supervisors were appointed. Secretary of War Baker appointed an advisory Library War Council to assist the Finance Committee. Chaired by Frank Vanderlip, president of the National City Bank of New York, the council was comprised of ten prominent citizens. Members of the council included Philander P. Claxton, U.S. Commissioner of Education; J. Randolph Coolidge, architect and trustee of the Boston Athenaeum; John H. Finley, New York State Commissioner of Education; and Mrs. Josiah E. Cowles, president of the General Federation of Women's Clubs.[4]

The campaign organization was two-tiered. At the state level, there was a divisional head and a state director (librarians); a salaried field director (fund raising expert); and a state war council. At the grass roots level, there was a campaign director (usually the local librarian) and a war council consisting of library trustees and ten prominent individuals from the local community. September 24-30 was designated as campaign week. To raise the $1 million, the Library War Council set the dollar quota at 5 percent of the local population, or one dollar for every twenty persons.[5]

The idea of a national financial campaign was not universally popular. Rossiter Johnson, editor and writer of popular histories, denounced the ALA's wartime plans in the *New York Times*. Convinced that the public would donate a sufficient number of books for the camps, Johnson believed that raising funds was unnecessary.[6] Frank Hill and Morgan J. O'Brien, chairman of the New York State Library War Council, replied that the gift books received to date were less than satisfactory, and that money was needed for library buildings and competent staff.[7] Undaunted, Johnson renewed his attack within a week, warning that the ALA's camp library system would create a needless bureaucracy and interpose red tape between soldiers and books. With overwhelming simplicity, he proposed that camp libraries be built in one day, that soldiers sort and shelve the books, and that no circulation records be maintained. Using this approach, Johnson asserted, would eliminate the need for trained librarians.[8]

Rushing into a fund drive only thirty days after creating the campaign organization left state and local organizers with a bewildering task. Some states managed to publicize the campaign widely; others did not. In most states, such groups as women's clubs, the Rotary, and the Council of National Defense assisted in the solicitation of funds. Not surprisingly, some rural areas were neglected. Complaints were leveled against the 5 percent quota in view of the fact that a country of 100,000,000 persons required only a 1 percent rate to collect $1 million. The South Dakota campaign, for example, was momentarily jeopardized when the state library announced a 1 percent quota; only after pressure from the field director was the goal raised to 5 percent.[9]

Considering the short time available to organize and conduct a campaign, the results were gratifying. By April 1, 1918, receipts amounted to $1,749,706 and campaign expenses were reported at only $74,865. Generally, the large urban areas fell short of their quotas, with New York City missing by $200,000. Intensive campaigning in the less populated areas enabled the drive to meet its goal. The Carnegie Corporation approved a $320,000 grant on September 14, 1917, which was later included in the total, but the ALA withheld this information from the public and instead encouraged prospective donors to believe that their contributors would be used for buildings as well as for books and services.[10]

The Library War Council, appointed to assist in the financial campaign, soon became the center of a controversy. Frank Vanderlip, the chairman, misconstrued his role, believing that he should not only advise on the fund drive, but also control expenditures and even influence book selection. And he did not think that the council should cease operations after the campaign, an opinion which distressed Putnam and Wyer.[11] Putnam told Frank Hill in December that Vanderlip's request for another meeting of the Library War Council would not be sanctioned by the War Service Committee. Annoyed over this decision, Hill advised Putnam:

> Please understand, my dear sir, that the Library War Council was appointed by the Secretary of War to assist the War Finance Committee and not the War Service Committee. Unfortunately, you are not acquainted with the history of this struggle since you lost interest in the early part of July. . . . You have all you can carry now and some of us think your load is a little heavier than you can bear.[12]

Hill's testy reply to Putnam was the opening salvo of an intermittent quarrel between two titans in the library profession. Competent, headstrong, and compulsively candid, Hill was devoted to the Library War Service. Putnam, too, was self-confident and determined. He did not give ground easily on matters of principle. Between the first fund drive and the second financial campaign in November 1918, Hill escalated his challenge to Putnam's authority.

Incoming ALA President William W. Bishop, presiding over the Executive Board meeting of July 5, 1918, was unsuspectingly drawn into the bitter controversy. At the meeting, Hill proposed a seemingly innocent resolution requesting the president to obtain from legal counsel an opinion as to the relations between the ALA, the Executive Board, the War Service Committee, and the general director of the Library War Service. In truth, Hill was disturbed over the extent of Putnam's administrative power as general director and the vesting of campaign funds in the name of the War Service Committee. Only a legal ruling, Hill believed, could settle the matter of how funds should be treated by the Association. Bishop realized the intensity of the dispute when he wrote John Cotton Dana suggesting that Hill ought to withdraw his grievance. Dana passed Bishop's letter along to Hill, who, in turn, furiously rebuked Bishop for prejudging the case: "It is not the first time that the gentleman's suavity has won in spite of the facts."[13]

As directed by the Executive Board, Bishop engaged counsel on August 8, 1918, selecting Henry C. Bulkey, a prominent Detroit attorney and a regent of the University of Michigan. Three weeks later, Bulkey submitted a report which upheld prior Executive Board decisions regarding powers delegated to the War Service Committee and the general director.[14] Hill was a sore loser and refused to pay the attorney's fee from Library War Service funds. Upon hearing of Hill's intransigence, James Wyer attempted to comfort Bishop:

> Mr. Hill's letter to you is outrageous. . . . It is a tight race between Mr. Putnam, Mr. Anderson, and myself as to which has stood the most from him. While not qualified to speak for the others, the reason I do it is because he is useful on the Committee, willing and able to do a heavy work that none of the rest of us will undertake, or probably could do as well. I therefore applaud your forebearance. . . .[15]

Hill could be irascible, even unforgivably abusive; but Wyer's complimentary estimate of Hill's value to the Library War Service was by no means inaccurate. And for the next fund drive, Hill was again drafted to lead the campaign.

Fearing that money from the first fund drive would be depleted by the fall of 1918, the War Service Committee initiated plans during

April 1918 for a second campaign. Initially, the Association had envisaged an independent campaign, but abandoned that idea in August and agreed to a combined appeal with the YMCA, the War Camp Community Service, and the Young Women's Christian Association. The three remaining agencies held out for separate fund drives, but were persuaded by President Wilson in early September to join with the others. The seven welfare societies affiliated with the Commission on Training Camp Activities thus agreed to conduct a unified fund drive—"the United War Work Campaign." A goal of $170.5 million was established for the unified campaign, the highest figure for a non-government fund drive in American history. The YMCA would receive the lion's share, $100 million, and the ALA, the Jewish Welfare Board, and the Salvation Army would each receive $3.5 million. Funds would be collected during the week of November 11.[16]

Although participating in a federated campaign gave the ALA the benefit of national exposure through a centralized publicity program, the Association still decided to establish a separate campaign staff and plunge ahead with a major publicity effort. Promotional activities for this campaign were far superior to those of the first one. Frank Stockbridge, editor of such publications as the *New York Evening Mail* and *Popular Mechanics,* was largely responsible for the improved quality of the publicity. He not only managed the ALA's promotional activities, but also held a key position on the national publicity committee of the United War Work Campaign. The first number of a new publication, *War Libraries,* was introduced on August 22. Stockbridge and others contributed glowing reports on the Library War Service to inspire rank-and-file librarians and to generate support from the general public.

Publicity materials available to libraries, heavily promoted in *War Libraries,* included posters, booklets, bookmarks, and press releases. Two broadsides containing short reports about camp libraries, entitled "Good Stories from Camp and Trench" and "More Stories from Camp and Trench," were widely distributed to the press. And since most newspapers mentioned each of the "seven sisters" in general pieces on the campaign, the Association received additional exposure in hundreds of press accounts. Altogether, 4,750,000 bookmarks and 47,500 posters were sent to libraries. Spokesmen for the Association traversed the country, telling the ALA story on the same platform with the six other agencies.[17]

Several interrelated arguments were used in the appeal for more funds. Books were no longer a military frill; nearly a year of wartime experience had convinced the Association that library service promoted social stability and encouraged educational self-improvement. Judson T. Jennings, the ALA state director in Washington, viewed books as "weapons" in the fighting man's arsenal. Reading served three main functions in modern warfare: contentment, efficiency, and education. Recreational literature, an antidote to the tedium and dehumanization of war, reduced soldiers' anxieties. Technical books were essential to waging a complex, technological war. Educational books stimulated soldiers to become better citizens and to improve their vocational skills before reentering civilian life.[18] Not all appeals were expressed in such subdued terms. The rhetoric of social purity and home-front patriotism was emphasized in this Denver newspaper solicitation:

> The Hohenzollern thinks he is fighting an American army and navy but this is a serious error; he's fighting the American home spirit, which is invincible. It means a morale that can't be shaken; and this is why we are going to win the war. Books for soldiers! Books to keep the minds of the boys clean and kindle their hearts with the warmth of the home circle. . . .[19]

Although the United War Work Campaign opened on November 11, the very day of Allied victory, the drive was still an immense success. The goal of $170 million was over-subscribed by $35 million. Eventually, the Association received $3.8 million. Without these funds, the wartime library program would have ceased shortly after the Armistice.[20]

An independent military library program would not have been possible without separate library facilities in each camp. Lacking its own funds, the Association turned to the Carnegie Corporation and submitted a grant application on July 8, 1917 for $320,000 to build and equip thirty-two camp libraries.[21] Carnegie officials were skeptical, however, about ALA plans for a central library facility. James Bertram, long-time private secretary to Andrew Carnegie, cautioned James Wyer that soldiers would not flock to libraries with the competition of other recreational services in the camps. Bertram believed that the ALA should modify building plans by reducing the seating accommodations and increasing the size of receiving and sorting areas.[22] Wyer took issue with Bertram. "We can scarcely believe that a building with accommodation for no more than two hundred readers will fail to be utilized to capacity in a camp with a population of thirty to forty thousand."[23] Wyer's prediction proved correct.

On September 14, the Carnegie Corporation approved the request for a matching grant of $320,000, with the stipulation that no building should exceed $10,000. But the vote was not unanimous (four to one), and subsequent contacts between Bertram and the War Service Committee over building modifications and other matters were strained.[24]

Building specifications for the camp libraries were prepared by Edward L. Tilton, a New York architect with previous library experience who volunteered his services in the summer of 1917. Originally, each single-story building was designed to be 120 feet long and 40 feet wide. Escalating construction costs necessitated reducing the length to 93 feet on twenty library facilities. Seating accommodations for 225 readers and shelving for approximately 14,000 volumes were provided in each library. A small area was set aside for living quarters, allowing the librarian to reside in the camp and to maintain liberal operating hours.[25]

Working under U.S. Army Quartermaster Corps guidelines, private firms constructed all of the camp libraries. Despite frustrating delays and material shortages, the first camp library (Camp Lewis, Washington) was opened on November 28, 1917, and the majority were completed by February 1918. Because of cost savings on some buildings, the Association was able to build thirty-six libraries from Carnegie funds. Four additional camp libraries/dispatch facilities were constructed from ALA funds during 1918 (Appendix I).[26]

Although substantial sums of money were collected in the financial campaigns, there was never enough money to purchase an adequate supply of books and magazines. To supplement the book purchases, the ALA conducted three book campaigns. These were held in September 1917, March 1918, and January 1919. Donations from these appeals were generous, and estimated at 4.2 million volumes. As in the fund drives, the publicity generated for the book collection campaigns brought the Association greater public recognition.

Guidelines for the first book campaign were prepared and published in August 1917. Fiction led the list of desired categories, but works of "stirring poetry," foreign language titles, technical works, and historical books were also solicited. Recognizing that the draft army would be comprised of men from every social strata, one Library War Service official asked librarians to relax their standards: "Don't be too fastidious or too 'high brow,' but help the humblest reader by accepting some titles which would not find a place in your library."[27] The rather amateurish publicity in this campaign consisted of suggestions to place posters in libraries, and to coordinate the appeal through local churches and community organizations. Twelve cities were selected as receiving and sorting centers from which the processed books were shipped to the camps by railroad at government expense. The campaign netted about 200,000 volumes.[28]

The demand for ALA books far exceeded the supply by January 1918. Of the 600,000 volumes distributed to the camps, only 100,000 had been purchased from proceeds of the first financial campaign. To alleviate this shortage, plans were developed for an intensive drive in March. Public libraries were the focal point of this campaign. Local librarians, designated as campaign directors, selected a "captain" of publicity to lead an advertising team. Additional personnel were chosen to coordinate collection activities with commercial organizations, patriotic societies, welfare groups, and churches. Local efforts were supplemented by a major publicity program at the national level. Two issues of the *War Library Bulletin* highlighted the drive; a dozen press releases flowed from Library War Service headquarters; and the first edition of Theodore Koch's illustrated pamphlet, *War Service of the American Library Association,* was widely disseminated.[29]

National press coverage, often incorporating ALA material, was extensive. At least several thousand notices appeared throughout the country. Under the frequent headline of "Books for Sammies," appeals stressed, as in the financial campaigns, that books were needed for morale, efficiency, and recreation. Camp librarians often contributed stories to nearby newspapers, informing citizens of the ALA war work in their region. Posters adorned every type of public place from store fronts and hotels to billiard halls and telegraph offices. Easily the most flamboyant advertisement of the book campaign appeared on the steps of the New York Public Library. A giant scaffold was erected, in the figure of a pyramid, upon which was stacked thousands of books. Library workers, megaphones hoisted, plied the public to donate books. A fifty-piece military band stirred the emotions with patriotic tunes and noted artist Charles B. Falls recreated a popular ALA poster on a fifteen foot canvass on the 5th Avenue side of the Library. Falls' poster, one of a half-dozen drawn for the Association at various times during the war, depicted a marine carrying an armful of books.[30]

Once collected, the gift books were prepared for shipment to state agencies, dispatch offices, and nearby camps. An ALA bookplate was affixed to each volume, book cards and pockets prepared, and a shelf-list card furnished for nonfiction titles. Fiction, it was anticipated would be shelved alphabetically, thus eliminating the need for an author catalog or a shelf list (a catalog arranged by classification notation). With reports still incomplete, the book drive was pronounced a success in early April 1918. Over 3,000,000 books had been donated, of which two-thirds were works of fiction. The final book campaign, conducted in the spring of 1919, was much less intensive than the second. About 500,000 volumes were collected and transported to Europe.[31]

Many of the books obtained in these drives were either in poor condition or, in the case of nonfiction and magazines, badly out of date. This fact, and the surging demand for nonfiction titles, eventually persuaded Library War Service officials to spend most of their funds on nonfiction and to depend upon public donations for fiction. In the early phase of camp library work, the need for nonfiction was not so apparent. After visiting several camps in 1917, Charles H. Brown of the Brooklyn Public Library notified Matthew Dudgeon that most soldiers wanted to read western novels, detective stories, and adventure tales. The War Service Committee's first list (September 1917) of approved books for camp libraries contained approximately 3,800 titles, of which 2,200, or 58 percent, were fiction.[32] Major reasons for the progressive shift to nonfiction were the informational needs of a mechanized war; the spirited competition for military promotions; and the vast educational program of the YMCA in Europe and America.

Commencing in September 1917, Charles Brown and several assistants at the Brooklyn Public Library developed guidelines for the acquisition and distribution of library materials. Publishers were asked, and in some cases pressured, to grant discounts of up to 50 percent (trade books only) on the promise of multiple copy orders. All of the major publishers agreed to this arrangement. Initially, books were shipped directly to the camps by the publishers. This cumbersome practice, coupled with the scarcity of Quartermaster rail space, caused frustrating delays. By Christmas, 1917, books were being shipped from publishers to the dispatch office at the New York Public Library and then routed to the camps.[33]

The need for centralization of the selection process soon became apparent and this responsibility was transferred to personnel at the Library of Congress in early 1918. Charles H. Compton, acting director of the Seattle Public Library and head of the Library War Service order department, described the operation in some detail. Approximately $70,000 per month was expended, an amount representing about 2,500 books a day. To ascertain book needs in the field, a checklist of 130 topics was prepared and sent to over 1,000 YMCA secretaries, chaplains, and camp commanders. Lists were collated and orders were usually dispatched within forty-eight hours. Exact figures for the total number of books purchased are not available. Just over 2,000,000 volumes were purchased through June 1919, and if the service to hospital

Carl H. Milam

Frank P. Hill

Pyramid of Books—New York Public Library

libraries and the merchant marine is counted, the figure probably exceeded 2.5 million.[34]

Various roles were assigned to the sixteen regional dispatch offices: receiving and sorting gift books; distributing books to domestic and overseas locations; and in several instances, supervising small camps in their area.[35] Originally established as distribution centers to serve camp libraries, the number of dispatch offices proliferated as the American force in Europe increased. The first dispatch office opened at the New York Public Library in the fall of 1917 and was followed by overseas offices in Hoboken, New Jersey (January 1918) and Newport News, Virginia (March 1918). By May 1919, the six dispatch offices making European shipments had processed 2,546,130 books and 219,963 magazines. Hoboken far outdistanced the others, with slightly over 1,000,000 volumes shipped to Europe.[36]

Sorting gift books was a continual preoccupation at the dispatch offices. According to James Hodgson of the dispatch office in the New York Public Library, about 20 percent of the donations were discarded prior to shipment. Many gifts were well intended, but of little value. Family Bibles, Greek grammars (circa 1830), nineteenth-century science texts, obscure annual reports, and "improper" books were among the culled items.[37] When Raney criticized overseas fiction shipments from the Boston dispatch office, the agent, C. O. S. Mawson, defended the quality of his selections while admitting that many donations were inferior. Mawson then favorably compared his shipments with those from the Hoboken office:

> Since you compare our selection unfavorably with that of the Hoboken office, might I remind you that I was in that office for some weeks during which time I personally sorted more than nine tenths of the books. . . . If you had handled the tons of books turned in unsorted from New York, books in every condition of filth and moral unfitness contributed from unsavory sections of New York City, you would have learned to appreciate the difference between such material and the excellent contributions of the New England libraries. The condition of some books was such that some of the ladies who prepared them grumbled continuously at having to come in contact with them.[38]

Recruiting and retaining competent personnel was the most immediate concern of Herbert Putnam in October 1917. The new general director inherited a staff of twelve camp librarians and a headquarters contingent of two men, George B. Utley and Matthew S. Dudgeon. Recruiting experienced librarians was especially important in the early phase of the program. Effective management by the headquarters staff and competent library service in the military camps were priority goals. If these objectives could be attained, the ALA would earn the respect of the Fosdick commission, the military authorities, and prospective volunteer librarians.[39]

Predictably, as the Library War Service expanded, the systemization of records and routines, and the specialization of functions became more pronounced. Functional specialization was very apparent in the headquarters by the summer of 1918, with supervisory positions for large camps, small camps and stations, overseas service, hospital libraries, educational work, book selection, and publicity. Another group, known as field representatives, acted as consultants to camp and hospital librarians throughout the nation. Further control was achieved through the appointment of nonsalaried regional supervisors who coordinated library activities within their geographical area. Three such supervisors, very active in their states, were Charles F. D. Belden in Massachusetts, Sarah Askew in New Jersey, and Milton J. Ferguson in California.[40]

Viewed in organizational terms, the Library War Service was a business-like activity with all of the components of a bureaucracy: centralized authority, functional specialization, procedural specification, and technical competence.[41] Management of a network of dispatch offices and a decentralized system of camp/hospital libraries required a larger and more authoritative bureaucracy than the Association had ever experienced. Development of a centralized organization undoubtedly contributed to the general effectiveness and efficiency of the Library War Service. Some librarians, however, viewed this consolidation of power as a threat to their professional autonomy.

Recruiting librarians for the Washington staff was easier than for the camp libraries because working at the Library of Congress was attractive and commanded relatively good salaries. Since some library organizers were in the field before the first financial campaign, they were not paid by the ALA. Many library boards allowed these men to serve from one to three months while retaining their salary. Camp librarians in the initial group were male, usually middle-aged, and well educated. A few women did supervise camp library services, but they were not given the title of camp librarian and did not reside in the camps until May 1918.[42]

Although many highly qualified librarians participated in the organizational phase of the war work, Putnam found it difficult to attract librarians of national stature. He was understandably elated when the eminent William H. Brett, seventy-two year old director of the Cleveland Public Library, agreed to serve as the dispatch agent at Newport News. By June 1918, 305 library workers had served in the Library War Service. Of this total, two-thirds were paid from ALA funds and one-third were non-salaried volunteers. Over 80 percent were affiliated with public or special libraries. During the period 1918 to 1920, between 1,100 and 1,200 persons, including librarians, assistants, and other support staff, were on the Library War Service payroll at various times.[43]

A persistent problem never fully overcome, was the rapid turnover of camp personnel. Few librarians remained in their jobs longer than six months. Another difficulty—competition from the military draft—reduced the pool of eligible librarians. On September 7, 1918, the Commission on Training Camp Activities announced that personnel of the seven welfare groups would be eligible for exemptions. Putnam hailed the decision as "very welcome," but others were critical.[44] Lloyd W. Josselyn, librarian at Camp Johnston (Florida), was vehemently opposed: "I urgently request our Headquarters to ask General Crowder to instruct Draft Boards not to honor this exemption claim. Let's not become more and more effeminate. We men have much to overcome as Librarians, and we need help rather than hindrance."[45] Later in the month, the commission reversed itself and informed the welfare groups that exemptions would not be granted to men in the highest draft classification.[46]

Blacks, German-Americans, and women faced varying degrees of discrimination in their attempts to join the Library War Service. A. C. Priestley, a college-educated black and an elementary school principal in New Orleans, applied for a position in May 1918. His application was supported by impressive recommendations from a U.S. Senator and a Congressman. In reply, Herbert Putnam evaded the race issue and belittled the Library War Service, telling Priestley that "our force is, in fact, a small one and very largely occupied with routine; opportunities for any appointments, except of a minor sort, are very infrequent."[47] Discouraging Priestley was realistic in that the military was segregated and the ALA did not maintain separate libraries for blacks. However, other agencies, principally the YMCA, did establish camp facilities to serve blacks.

German-American applicants were similarly discouraged. William F. Frerichs was a naturalized American citizen born in Germany and librarian of McMinnville College, Oregon. The Library War Service approached Frerichs' application with great caution, as evidenced by this comment to one of his references: "You can readily see that the employment of any native German is a matter of some risk, and we feel it very necessary to safeguard the matter in every possible way."[48] Frerichs, despite three letters attesting to his loyalty, was not accepted.

Female librarians were never excluded from the war work, but for many months they were denied the opportunity to serve as camp librarians. By itself, this situation might have been tolerated and the disappointment repressed. But the Library War Service policy barring women from the camps was vigorously challenged, first in private correspondence, and then in open forum at the Association's annual conference in 1918. Long a subordinated majority in the library profession, female librarians became increasingly assertive, even defiant.[49]

Many American women came to view the war as a unique opportunity to consolidate past gains and to break new ground in a male-dominated society. Eager to serve, women joined the labor force in unprecedented numbers and contributed their time to a broad range of volunteer activities. The federal government recognized women by creating a Committee on Women's Defense within the Council of National Defense and by establishing a Women's Bureau in the Department of Labor. After years of opposition, President Wilson endorsed the suffrage amendment in 1918. Originally employed as temporary replacements, women performed magnificently in many traditionally male occupations. Although some gains were eroded after the war, the precedents and accomplishments were undeniable.[50]

It was hardly surprising, therefore, that several female librarians resented what they considered to be an exclusionary policy. Foremost among the disaffected librarians was Beatrice Winser, Dana's assistant at the Newark Free Public Library. Winser, a librarian for twenty-eight years, bypassed ALA officials and wrote to Secretary of War Baker in February 1918. She could not understand why women resided in camp hospitals and supervised hostess houses, while female librarians were barred from the camps.[51] Obviously embarrassed by the Winser protest, Putnam replied to Raymond Fosdick that several women were already serving as unpaid assistants in the camp libraries. And then, gratuitously, Putnam observed that ''if a woman can serve tea in a hostess house, there would seem to be no reason why she could not serve books in a library.'' Greater utilization of women librarians was promised in the future.[52] Unrepentant, Putnam was less cordial to Winser. He noted that the Library War Service had never adopted a policy of exclusion and recalled that the Fosdick commission had decided against using women in the camps in October 1917. Putnam inaccurately stated that the War Department barred women. Actually, the issue was left to local commanders and a top-level prohibition never existed.[54]

Putnam and the War Service Committee had been conditioned by the long-time passivity of many female librarians, the opposition of some female library leaders to women in camps, and the reports of early camp library organizers. At the time of the Winser imbroglio, Sara Askew, the ALA representative in New Jersey, told Carl Milam that it would be "absolutely beyond reason" to send a woman to Camp Merritt.[54] Malcolm G. Wyer, organizer of the library at Camp Logan in Houston, Texas, did not believe that female librarians could have coped with the "hardships and uncertainties" of the organizational phase of the camp work.[55]

The issue was aired at the Saratoga Springs, New York, conference in the summer of 1918. Seven women, including Winser and the ALA's first woman president, Theresa Elmendorf, petitioned the War Service Committee to amend the policy regarding the utilization of women. Chairman Wyer temporized, thanking the women for their concern, but refusing to promise major changes. He tried to mollify the protesters by pointing out that of the 305 persons who had already served in the Library War Service, 69 were women and 236 were men. But the speeches went on.[56] Finally, an exasperated Putnam spoke to the membership. He welcomed the petition, if only "because of the *manly* expressions the discussions of it has evoked" [italics in original]. But he was displeased with the protestors' implication that those female librarians already serving in the Library War Service were doing less than significant work.[57] Unaccountably, Putnam failed to mention that Blanche Galloway had been assigned in May 1918 to the Pelham Bay (New York) Naval Training Station. She was the first female librarian to direct an ALA military library.

It is difficult to assess the impact of the Winser protest and the Saratoga petition. The fine example of many female YMCA and Red Cross workers in Europe, coupled with the relaxation of regulations after the Armistice, probably contributed more to the greater use of female librarians than anything else. By the summer of 1919, in any event, women were in charge of eight camp libraries, seven women had served as field representatives, and women held most of the key positions on the Washington staff.[58]

THREE

'Over Here':
Domestic Service

Matthew Dudgeon told camp librarians in November 1917 that the Library War Service marked "the beginning of a new era in the development of libraries."[1] Excited over the prospect of elevating the profession's status, Dudgeon hoped to instill a strong sense of mission among librarians:

> The present movement is the opportunity for which we have been waiting. It is an opportunity to demonstrate to the MEN of America— both those in military service and those in the higher circles of governmental activities—that library work is a profession; that we librarians are in this work because it offers expression to our ideals; that we are not only professional men and women, but that we are business people, who can engage in a nation-wide undertaking from a national point of view.[2]

Dudgeon clearly wanted to erase the notion that librarians were passive and effeminate. Grafting the corporate ideal of efficient management to the bibliographical expertise of librarianship was the best way to win public esteem.

Dudgeon's impassioned rhetoric aside, the provision of library service to soldiers in the United States was a critical test of the ALA's professionalism and resolve. If the Association had faltered, the opportunity to serve in Europe and elsewhere would have been foreclosed. And the failure would have been a humiliating admission of professional inadequacy to the American public. While failure was never imminent, success was not easily achieved.

Existing army facilities were utterly inadequate to house the 1,000,000 men soon to be drafted. To billet the men, thirty-two soldier-cities were needed in ninety days. Construction of the cantonments and camps, sixteen each, began in June 1917. Draftees in the National Army were scheduled to occupy cantonments, installations with permanent wooden barracks. Experienced militia men in the National Guard, on the other hand, were assigned to the camps. Located in the South, the camps were temporary posts consisting of tent accommodations.[3]

Secretary Baker personally supervised the building program, contending with the inevitable pork-barrel politics and profit-hungry contractors. Each camp housed one division of between 30,000 and 50,000 soldiers. Standardized to a large extent, the typical camp was built along a three-mile street lined with two-story barracks or tents. Behind the living quarters were all of the medical, sanitary, and communication facilities needed to support the residents. Notwithstanding material shortages and labor strikes, the thirty-two camps were declared finished on October 15, 1917. It had taken slightly more than ninety days to complete quarters for 1,372,718 men, a feat unrivalled in construction history.[4]

Never before had so many Americans from so many different social strata and ethnic backgrounds lived and trained together. The "typical" recruit was a bachelor draftee between the ages of twenty-one and twenty-three. Army medical records indicate that he stood 5'7 1/2" tall and weighed 141 1/2 pounds. Eighteen percent were foreign born and 10 percent were black. American soldiers spoke more than fifty languages, including Austronesian, Gaelic, and American Indian dialects.[5]

After September 1, the men started pouring into the camps. It was a lucky recruit who received a uniform, a warm blanket, and a rifle. By December most of the nation was suffering from sub-zero temperatures. Inadequate heating and sanitation facilities contributed to serious outbreaks of contagious diseases. As outraged parents complained and newspaper editorials inveighed against the War Department, the Congress activated five separate investigations relating to the camps and to the military supply system.[6]

Camp librarians were deployed throughout the nation before permanent library facilities were constructed. The location and character of the temporary libraries depended upon the generosity of post commanders and the cooperation of the other welfare agencies. At Camp Sherman (Ohio), Burton E. Stevenson, director of the nearby Chillicothe Public Library, was warmly received. Stevenson, probably the first to organize a camp library, had secured library space in two YMCA buildings by August 15. Even the commander's daughter (a Pratt Institute Library School graduate) pitched in by supervising the technical work of preparing the books for circulation. From Camp Shelby in Misisippi, Whitman Davis reported a less congenial reception. After several days of frantic cajoling, he was given temporary use of a small, abandoned canteen which had a dirt floor and no windows. Davis made the best of it and was soon dispensing ALA books in huts maintained by the YMCA and the Knights of Columbus.[7]

Library service was introduced to Camp Logan (Texas) by Malcolm G. Wyer. On leave from the directorship of the University of Nebraska Library, Wyer guided the early library work at Logan with exceptional skill. For several weeks after his arrival on November 20, he lived in a YMCA hut and dined with the enlisted men and the officers. From these contacts Wyer learned about the soldiers' training regimen, reading habits, and library needs. Wyer's first task was to achieve a measure of bibliographic control over the 4,000 books scattered throughout the camp. In most of the buildings he found the shelves in disarray, no one to care for the books, and primitive or nonexistent circulation procedures. Within several weeks, Wyer and several assistants had labelled the books, affixed book pockets and cards, developed an accession system, and furnished charging trays to each branch library.[8]

As a part of a general survey of welfare agency operations in the camps, Raymond Fosdick authorized Harold Braddock to evaluate the progress of library service. After completing an inspection tour of eleven southern camps (October-November 1917), Braddock submitted his report to Fosdick and Putnam. None of the camps had a permanent library building and seven camps did not have a resident librarian. When books and magazines were found, they were frequently out-of-date and unprocessed. At Camp Sheridan (Alabama), Braddock found the ALA library in an abandoned shack filled with old magazines and 4,000 gift books. The situation was even more dismal at Camp Shelby: no building, no new books, no automobile, and one inadequate assistant. Unpaid to date, the librarian was ready to abandon camp library work and return to his regular post. With salaries of $100 per month, Braddock was skeptical that the ALA could attract and retain competent librarians for the camps.

Noting the distinction between assembling a collection of books and providing library service, Braddock complained that the ALA had not yet contributed much in the way of professional service. The Association "has the opportunity of a century" and it has not placed itself "on record as being able . . . to make this distinction." Braddock recommended enlargement of the ALA's Washington staff and the assignment of librarians to specific areas of responsibility. He also urged Library War Service officials to visit the camps before taking corrective action. Unsparing and direct, Braddock did not even concede the Association's inexperience with such activities and the superior financial resources of the other welfare groups.[9]

Shaken by the findings and tone of the report, Putnam reacted by challenging it *seriatum*. He assured Fosdick that librarians were now present and library buildings were under construction at each of the camps inspected by Braddock. Putnam wanted Fosdick to know that he appreciated the facts which Braddock noted, even if he was aware of them; however, he deeply resented Braddock's "impertinent and shallow" reflections on those facts. Putnam was especially infuriated over Braddock's successful attempt to elicit critical statements from one of the camp librarians about Library War Service policies. The librarian, Joseph L. Wheeler, was interviewed by Braddock at Camp Sheridan. According to Putnam, Wheeler recalled that "Braddock drew him on to exploit grievances against Headquarters, until he had done so to a degree of which he is heartily ashamed." Wheeler told Putnam that Braddock even made a "scandalous insinuation against [Putnam] personally."[10] Putnam's defensive posture could scarcely mask the essential truth of Braddock's findings. As of November 1917, the Association's military libraries were little more than book depots.

James Wyer made the first extensive assessment of the camp library system in March 1918. Although only four months had elapsed between Braddock's caustic report and Wyer's inspection, many improvements were evident. One hundred full-time employees staffed the thirty-five camp libraries. For the fourteen major camps visited by Wyer, book collections ranged from 9,000 to 25,000 volumes, with the average library holding 17,000 books. Assistance was often available to the librarian, usually work details consisting of conscientious objectors, prisoners, or the physically disqualified. Where the book stock was adequate, volumes were distributed to other welfare agencies, the camp hospital, and individual barracks. Wyer found nothing but praise for the Washington staff. Only two deficiencies were noted—the general need for more books and the desirability of more publicity within the camps.[11] Wyer's findings were corroborated by a member of Fosdick's commission, who remarked that the commission's district directors were reporting "most enthusiastically" about the "well managed and liberally patronized" camp libraries in their areas.[12]

Two months later Frank Hill, at the request of the War Service Committee, toured ten southern camps. His report was not as optimistic as Wyer's. Of the ten camp librarians, only five had professional backgrounds. Publicity within the camps was still ineffective. Book collections were over-stocked with dated and duplicate titles. In contrast to the compliments about the Washington staff received by Wyer, Hill noted considerable resentment. Complaints levelled at the headquarters included delays in answering correspondence, burdensome reporting procedures, and insufficient recognition of local needs.[13] The divergent findings of Wyer and Hill may be ascribed to several factors. Different camps were inspected by each individual; camp librarians may have been more reluctant to share negative comments with Wyer because of his position as chairman of the War Service Committee; and Hill was by nature the more critical of the two.

Most camp librarians and state organizers accepted the centralization of authority in Washington. Sarah B. Askew resisted it. As secretary of the New Jersey Public Library Commission, Askew coordinated library service to more than thirty military camps and stations. Aggressive and resourceful, Askew was intensely proud of her war work. She persistently queried the Washington staff about lines of authority, funds, shipping procedures, and camp personnel. Askew never lost a battle with headquarters over the appointment of librarians in New Jersey camps.[14]

During January 1918, Carl Milam attempted to modify some New Jersey procedures. Instead of all libraries reporting to the state library commission, Milam designated some libraries to report directly to the ALA. Askew drew the line.[15] To accept Milam's request would dilute her statewide authority and would divert books from the New Jersey camps. Deferential toward Milam, yet firm in her distrust of the ALA, Askew dissented:

> I frankly think too great centralization in Washington will be a very great mistake. I am sorry to say that to most libraries the ALA is an awesome far off body to whom they don't owe a very great amount of allegiance. . . . Now you say this is the time to bring ALA closer. No, it isn't Mr. Milam . . . this matter of recognition of ALA was rubbed into us so much during the [first] campaign for money that we began to feel that the ALA would perhaps rather have less money and more recognition. Nothing so big as this can be managed from a central point without a great deal of red tape, without loss of all of the human touch, without loss of interest, without taking the pleasures out of it. Please, don't federalize us. Let's be human and efficient.[16]

Milam deferred to Askew and allowed her to retain the existing reporting procedures. At least in New Jersey, Milam was checkmated and he never intruded again.

Askew's victory for home rule was an exception. On most matters, the Washington staff was the final arbiter. Librarians were not accustomed to decisive leadership from their professional association; and some, like Sarah Askew, selectively opposed the ALA's assertion of power. Nevertheless, if reasonably uniform procedures in the camps were considered desirable, and if reading matter was to be distributed equitably among the geographically dispersed camp libraries, then strong leadership from the Association was imperative.

By July 1918, when the Association convened in Saratoga Springs, New York, most of the early problems had been resolved. Conceding a slow start during the fall of 1917, the general director reported that "the present situation is different."[17] Just over 2.1 million books had been distributed to domestic service points, including 41 large camps, 237 small camps, 116 vessels, and 91 hospitals. Within the large camps, 1,323 library branches and stations were maintained. A travelling library system operated out of San Antonio and El Paso to supply books for the thousands of men stationed along the Mexican border.[18] Although imperfections in administration and shortages of library materials still persisted, the camp library program had attained operational maturity and broad-based acceptance.

Between November 1917 and March 1919, the Library War Service staff issued fifteen informational circulars pertaining to the management of camp libraries. In June 1918, the circulars issued to that point were edited and published as the *Camp Library Handbook*.[19] Suggestive rather than prescriptive, the *Handbook* touched on every aspect of camp library operation, from the technical routines of sorting and preparing books to the installation of drinking fountains. Most of the recommendations derived from the actual experiences of camp librarians. Although the libraries were quite similar with respect to collections, personnel, and services, local variations were common. Putnam often pointed to the pragmatic nature of the military library program: "We chose to experiment; prescribing upon theory as little as possible."[20]

Camp library buildings were plain wooden structures, conforming to the architectural style adopted for the cantonments. Most of the libraries were painted a "tawny yellow" color and equipped with a roof sign which was illuminated at night. The interiors were well lighted, and coal-burning stoves supplied heat in the winter months. Each library was supplied with a government telephone and a Ford runabout. This small truck, or "jitney," was used for deliveries within the camp and for picking up books from nearby libraries.[21]

The typical camp library was staffed by three full-time employees and volunteer assistants. Since camp libraries were generally open fourteen hours a day, the librarian's job was a demanding one. Camp librarians were barely distinguishable from their military comrades. Association uniforms were closely patterned after military apparel. Winter uniforms for the male librarians were forest green and featured army-style hats, coats, and puttees. Gray field cotton was prescribed for the summer months. Embroidered armbands and "A.L.A." collar insignia pins bedecked the uniform. Female librarians wore high-necked blouses, ties, skirts, jackets, and Panama hats. Smart appearance, proper bearing, and personal probity were stressed. Library personnel were expected to conduct themselves in the same manner as military officers. [22]

As of June 1918, the total number of books in the forty-one main camps was 1,051,693. The average number of volumes per library was 25,651. Camp Upton (New York) claimed the largest collection, 50,170 volumes. Fourteen camps had fewer than 25,000 books. Approximately 65 percent of each library consisted of fiction titles. A large percentage of the nonfiction works were technical treatises. About 20 percent of each collection consisted of books purchased by the Library War Service. Some of these titles were selected by the Washington staff and others were requested by camp librarians. Whenever possible, the Library of Congress honored interlibrary loan requests from the camps. [23]

Each library subscribed to thirty-eight periodicals and received another thirteen magazines provided without cost by their publishers. Titles available in the periodical collections included *Cavalry Journal, Harper's, North American Review, Scientific American,* and *Scribner's.* Supplementing their regular subscriptions were the tons of magazines donated by the public, known as "Burleson magazines" after the Postmaster General. Citizens could affix a one cent stamp to a used magazine and return it to the post office, which then routed it to a camp. Over 5,000,000 Burleson magazines had reached the camps by the summer of 1918. Sometimes a camp received two or three dozen sacks of Burleson magazines per day. [24]

When the Library War Service was first contemplated, extensive record-keeping systems and elaborate card catalogs were not envisioned. As the program developed, camp libraries adopted, often in simplified form, most of the technical routines employed in civilian libraries. Formal accession records were not required, but each camp tabulated the total number of books in the collection, adjusting the figure for additions and discards. The Decimal Classification, devised by Melvil Dewey in 1876, was used by every library. For nonfiction works, shelf lists were maintained, and titles were arranged on the shelves by call number. For fiction titles, author catalogs were employed. Each book was provided with a book pocket and card, and stamped to indicate ALA ownership. No separate registry of borrowers was kept.[25]

Simplified procedures were established for the books distributed to branches and stations. Branch libraries consisted of collections with at least 300 books which were placed in the various welfare agency buildings. Books were circulated under the supervision of these agencies. Another type of collection, the station collection, consisted of 50 to 100 books. These collections were distributed to individual barracks, mess halls, police quarters, prison stockades, and elsewhere. Usually, station collections were housed in wooden cases and the books were charged out by the soldiers themselves.[26]

Barriers between books and soldiers were minimal. Every camp library maintained an open-shelf collection. When a soldier wished to withdraw a book, he signed the book card, indicated his company or regiment, and gave the book card to the librarian. The card and the book were date-stamped, and the transaction was completed. Books circulated for seven days. The Association adhered to an honor system without fines and expected the same from the agencies which received its books. However, local commanders and YMCA secretaries occasionally imposed fines. Placing Association books under the care of welfare groups was an imperfect arrangement. In the smaller camps especially, books distributed to the YMCA were often slighted. Some educational secretaries imposed petty rules restricting use of the books, failed to record circulations, and neglected to send overdue notices. Near the end of the war, the Association and the YMCA made a concerted effort to remedy these problems.[27]

Camp libraries provided many services: support of the educational programs conducted by the military and the YMCA; general reference; and individual reader guidance. Of the services provided by the camp libraries, none surpassed the commitment to the military's educational curricula. Technologically more sophisticated than previous conflicts, World War I required a literate army comprised of numerous specialties. As Raymond Fosdick observed, "the training camp of today is not essentially different from a big university."[28] Soldiers were sometimes referred to as "students in khaki." In order to master the various military specialties and to pass the proficiency examinations for promotions, soldiers needed books and journals in unprecedented quantities. During the war the demand for technical literature was very heavy, while after the Armistice there was a shift in interest to more vocationally oriented titles.

The YMCA sponsored an extensive program of religious and educational activities. Lectures and discussion groups were devoted to such topics as war issues, citizenship, Americanization, art appreciation, literacy, and vocational training. Camp library collections were available to supplement YMCA resources in all of these areas. The Association was particularly committed to serving illiterate and foreign-born soldiers.

Although reliable figures are wanting as to the number of illiterates drafted, the degree of illiteracy alarmed both the military authorities and the welfare organizations. Soldiers of foreign extraction as well as native Americans were unable to read and write. Many of the native-born, white and black, came from the Appalachian and southern regions of the country. A Library War Service publication poignantly alluded to the "tragic" ignorance of these illiterate soldiers.[29] Literacy programs were organized by the army and the YMCA, and the ALA furnished primers and simplified texts to all of the camps.

World War I polarized the country's attitudes toward the immigrant population. Prior to 1914, efforts to Americanize the foreign born were usually motivated by a liberal, humanitarian impulse. Social workers in the urban settlement houses provided a receptive environment, tempering the pull of assimilation with respect for the Old World heritage. After 1914, liberal Americanism lost ground to the "100 percenters," those who demanded greater national cohesiveness.[30]

Librarians generally endorsed the liberal approach to Americanization, encouraging the foreign born to read English while supplying them with transitional literature in their native languages.[31] The Association supported Americanization programs in the camps, dispensing books, magazines and newspapers in over twenty-five languages. Frank L. Tolman arrived at Camp Upton wary of the "varied foreign elements." How could these "socialists, anarchists and pacificists," who harbored "antagonistic thoughts" and cherished "different national sentiments," be assimilated? He soon changed his mind, crediting military discipline and library service as factors contributing to the "transformation of this mass of human material into a splendid army."[32] Crediting the camp library as a major catalyst, acculturating the foreign born into the army and the mainstream of American society was undoubtedly excessive. At the very least, however, camp librarians welcomed the foreign born and furnished literature which enabled them to pursue language study in the classroom and during their leisure hours.

From all evidence, the camp libraries were popular with the soldiers. Library hours were generous, usually from 8:00 AM to 10:00 PM, seven days a week. Officers and men mingled in the same room. Soldiers could read, smoke, and write letters. Many soldiers appreciated the camp library as a haven from the regimen of the drill field, the tedium of the classroom, and the clamor of the barracks. A soldier at Camp Devens (Massachusetts) frequented the ALA library because "the barrack's social room . . . is certainly no decent place to read, let alone trying to do any studying."[33] "I'll be hanged if this isn't civilization," effused a regular army sergeant during his first visit to the Camp Funston (Kansas) Library.[34] An army officer wrote to Frederick Keppel that the ALA library was the only place in camp "without the 'God-bless-you' atmosphere of the other welfare organizations."[35]

Attendance and circulation figures further attest to the heavy use of the camp libraries, and they provide a barometer of the soldiers' reading interests. On a Tuesday evening in April 1918, the Camp Greene (North Carolina) Library reported 320 soldiers crowded into the reading room, many of them seated on the floor. Over 1,000 men had visited the library that day.[36] Less than a month after the Camp Kearny (California) Library opened, December 31, 1917, attendance exceeded 1,500 during a weekend day.[37] Other camp libraries reported similar attendance rates. May 1918 circulation figures for the central library and supervised branches were 14,116 at Camp Lewis and 17,076 at Kelly Field (Texas).[38]

In most camp libraries, the demand for nonfiction exceeded the call for fiction. During 1918, the Great Lakes Naval Training Station recorded 30,164 loan transactions for the central library. Of these loans, 60.5 percent were nonfiction.[39] Similarly, an eight-day circulation analysis at Camp Wadsworth (South Carolina) in April 1918, disclosed that 1,994 books had circulated, of which 64 percent were nonfiction.[40] These circulation statistics did not take into account the heavy use of materials within the libraries and did not include the dozens of smaller outlets within the camps. Since the nonfiction segment of the typical library collection was small, approximately 35 percent, the demand for these works was disproportionately high.

Reading preferences of the soldiers were conditioned by their educational background, military course of study, and recreational interests. The three categories of nonfiction in most demand were technical works related to military training, reference books about Europe, and personal narratives of the war. Especially popular war narratives were Arthur G. Empey's *Over the Top*, James W. Gerard's *My Four Years in Germany,* and Ian Hay's *First Hundred Thousand.* Heavily read titles included such fiction as Zane Grey's western novels, Edgar Rice

Burroughs' Tarzan series, and Jack London's adventure stories; detective stories by A. Conan Doyle and Edward Oppenheim; humorous works by Mark Twain and Irvin S. Cobb; essays by Ralph Waldo Emerson; plays by George Bernard Shaw; and poetry by Robert W. Service and Rudyard Kipling.[41]

Soldiers' comments about books, librarians, and camp libraries were eagerly recorded. Dozens of these comments and anecdotes were regularly published in the *War Library Bulletin* and released as press notices to newspapers and magazines.[42] More often than not in these accounts, librarians highlighted the fact that a soldier called for the plays of Ibsen, the sonnets of Shakespeare, the essays of Plato, or some other classic. Although serious literature circulated far less often than technical works and light fiction, most librarians could not restrain themselves from public testimony of their high cultural standards. Some books were simply better than others.[43]

Some books, however, never reached the camp libraries; and if they did, were promptly removed by the librarian. Beginning in July 1918, officials in the War Department ordered certain titles banned from the camps. The Association, ironically, had been practicing self-censorship from the outset of the war, and willingly collaborated with the War Department in the removal of books. Although the War Department's censorship program was intended as a covert operation, the names of the proscribed books were released in September. After several newspapers printed the lists, the Association was called upon to defend its selection practices.

The Albany, New York, *Knickerbocker-Press* reported the first episode of censorship on February 18, 1918, by noting that three war books written by Paul Koenig, Count Ernst von Reventlow, and Hrolf von Dewitz, were barred from circulating at the Camp Upton Library. The books in question had been received from the New York State Library. Apparently the volumes had been banned by local military authorities since James Wyer said he did not know why the books had been withdrawn. Wyer defended the Koenig book, denying the allegation that it was a propaganda work favorable to Germany.[44]

Within a week the War Department asked Herbert Putnam why Herbert Bayard Swope's *Inside the German Empire* was circulating in the camp libraries. The book would not be removed, Putnam said, since Swope was a Pulitzer Prize winner, the book was not pro-German, and soldiers needed to understand the enemy. Putnam promised, however, to "remove any really objectional books" in the future.[45] A month later Putnam confided to George H. Tripp of the New Bedford (Massachusetts) Public Library that some books should

Camp Funston Library (Kansas)

Library Delivery Truck (Camp Mills, New York)

Soldier Reading

Sailor Reading

not be sent to the camps. "The question is not [one] of exclusion, but merely one of selection," Putnam asserted, "and that is the only safe attitude for us."[46]

A sharp-eyed newspaperman on the *Detroit News* discovered in late March that the Library War Service was diverting some gift books from the camps. From a publicity pamphlet issued by the Association, he learned that books by Émile Zola, Guy de Maupassant, and Alphonse Daudet were being withheld by sorters at the New York Public Library.[47] Indignant over this practice, he composed a scathing editorial:

> The deadly censorship fever spreads more rapidly in war time than any other mental disease, and America is especially subject to it. In peace days our national literature was puritanized and mollycoddled practically out of existence by the Comstockery of the post office department and the public libraries. Now the camp libraries are threatened by the same malady. It is more important that they be saved from it than that some notion of democracy be injected into the municipal libraries. In an American city one can go across the street and buy or order a book that the public library has refused to furnish. In military camps no such opportunity is open.
>
> Every man and woman should see to it that the books intended for the nation's fighting men go to those men, and not to the junk pile of some 'library expert' who thinks he is competent to act as censor over the minds of men whose lives guarantee his security.
>
> It is not easy to comprehend the nature of egotism that permits this 'assistant' or any other to set himself up as an 'intellectual dietician.' This is supposed to be a war for democracy. The fundamental theory of democracy is that the people—not the superior people, but all the people—have the right to rule themselves. Certainly, it seems that we should put this notion into practice, at least to the extent of assuming that a man fighting for democracy has a right to choose his own reading matter.[48]

The writer's libertarian plea did not influence subsequent actions of the Association.

Pressure from the War Department to cleanse libraries of pacifist and pro-German titles intensified during the spring and summer of 1918. Apprehensive that enemy agents might glean technical secrets from *Popular Science* magazine, the chief of the army's Military Intelligence Branch asked the Association not to distribute the periodical to domestic camps or overseas. Army officials finally relented after the Library War Service convinced them of the futility of banning the publication. The men would get it through other channels anyway.[49]

On another occasion, the War Department contacted the Commission on Training Camp Activities, perhaps believing that the commission would exert pressure on the Association. That belief was not misplaced. The book in question, Henri Barbusse's *Under Fire,* had circulated at the Camp Sherman Library. Since the book was being serially published by George S. Viereck, a German apologist, the War Department considered it pernicious propaganda and wanted it removed from the camps. Putnam complied with the request and assured the commission that the Barbusse volume was no longer being issued and would be destroyed wherever it surfaced. "We shall take prompt measures" to eliminate any titles regarded as "objectionable," he concluded.[50] The capitualtion was complete.

On July 31, 1918, the Association issued a list of fourteen books to be removed from the camp libraries. The request, Library War Service officials said, was made by the War Department and full compliance was expected. Camp librarians were asked to maintain a constant vigil, especially for pacifist works published by religious sects and philanthropic societies. No publicity was to be given to the removal program. Five more lists were issued by the Library War Service during August.[51]

Since the press had leaked some of the banned titles in early September, the "Army Index" was officially released by the War Department in two installments later in the month. Altogether, eighty books and pamphlets were banned from the camps (Appendix II). The *New York Tribune* reported that the books had been carefully read by military censors who pronounced some titles as "vicious German propaganda" and others as either "salacious" or "morbid."[52] The list of censored titles was highly selective, omitting many possible candidates. Hundreds of pro-German and pacifist books and pamphlets had been published since 1914.[53]

Apart from the alleged pro-German or pacifist bias of the books, no pattern is discernible. Neither the backgrounds of the authors nor the publishers themselves provide a clue as to why certain books were selected for the list and others excluded. Among the banned books were *Understanding Germany* by Max Eastman; *War and Waste* by David Starr Jordan; *The Heel of War* by George B. McClellan; *England or Germany?* by Frank Harris; and *Why War?* by Frederic C. Howe. The authors defy occupational classification. Eastman was a socialist and editor of the *Masses*; Jordan was the former president of Stanford University; McClellan, son of the famed Civil War general, was a lieutenant colonel in the AEF; Harris was a professional writer and editor; and Howe was a civic reformer and Commissioner of Immigration, Port of New York. Considering the entire list, no publisher

53

was immune from inclusion. Small firms sympathetic to the German point of view, such as the Fatherland Corporation and Open Court Publishing Co. were heavily represented, but the more familiar names of Century, Macmillan, and Scribner's also dotted the list.[54]

Editorial opinion regarding the War Department's censorship was overwhelmingly favorable. The *Boston Evening Transcript* offered this appraisal of the banned books:

> Here is a group of old friends! The pro-German whose motive was money, and the pro-German whose motive may have been less selfish, tho none the less sinister. The addle-headed pacifist, working hand-in-hand with the paid servants of absolutism and militarism, and play-ing—innocently or not—their game for them. The German-born pro-fessors, obedient to Potsdam, and ready to snarl at England. The Amer-ican-born professors, their opinion warped and their historical judg-ment corrupted by a lunch with Wilhelm II—and a ribbon to stick in their coats. The professional Irish patriot—always remaining safe in New York or Boston, but very warlike against England, and eager to ally himself with the Hun—in the name of liberty! What a crew they are![55]

Asked to comment on the ban, Edwin H. Anderson of the New York Public Library remarked that "if Satan wrote a pro-German book we should want it for our reference-shelves." But, he quickly added, objectionable books had been removed from general circulation since the beginning of the war. A spokesman for the Association conceded that some inflammatory pamphlets had reached camp libraries, but denied that any books on the army's list were circulating in the camps. Personnel of the Library War Service were "trained librarians of proven loyalty" who were "constantly on the alert against insidious at-tempts to corrupt our fighting men."[56]

There was almost a complete blackout concerning the banning in the library press. Disregarding the ALA's directive to suppress the matter, however, Indiana's *Library Occurrent* listed the books and rec-ommended that all public libraries withdraw the suspect books.[57] Other organizations were pleased by the ban. The American Protective League advised readers of its bulletin, the *Spy Glass*, that the camp li-brary ban should be extended to public libraries as well.[58]

Toward the end of the war, various government officials ques-tioned the desirability of continuing the censorship program. Fred-erick Keppel wanted to restore some unfairly censored titles. Even George Creel regarded the suppression of certain books as "absurd."[59] Newton Baker's role in the censorship affair is unclear. He may not have known about the zealous officers in the army's Military Intelligence Branch and Morale Division who issued the various lists. And he was in France in September 1918, the month when the press gave so much coverage to the book banning. Baker rescinded the censorship policy a week after the cessation of hostilities, declaring that "American soldiers could be trusted to read whatever any other citizens could be trusted to read."[60]

The Association's assent to wartime censorship restrictions is explainable, if not excusable. Compliance by the Association with the War Department's censorship policy did not involve a special concession or require the suspension of a codified professional principle. Censorship was extensive in civilian libraries during neutrality and the war years. This paternalism was easily transferred to the more authoritarian environment of the military. Other professional groups and scholars, too, succumbed to the nationalist spirit of the times. Several outstanding historians, for example, wrote propaganda tracts for the government which clearly compromised any claims to scholarly objectivity. The chance to demonstrate the value of books and libraries on such a grand scale might never occur again. To have challenged the military authorities almost certainly would have jeopardized this opportunity. A challenge, if ever considered, did not materialize. As late as April 1919, the "intellectual dieticians" were still recommending the removal of books from camp libraries.[61]

The signing of the Armistice on November 11, 1918 did not signal the end of the domestic war work. Demobilization was slow, especially in Europe. At home, just over 1.6 million men had received discharges by March 1919. Embarkation began from France in November 1918, but the monthly flow of returning soldiers did not reach its peak until June 1919. By that month slightly more than 2.7 million AEF soldiers had been mustered out. Two months later only 40,000 American troops remained in Europe. Between the Armistice and the fall of 1919, the Association pursued the objectives of reorienting camp library services toward a vocational emphasis and dismantling the camp library system in preparation for the assumption of control by the military departments.[62]

Pending discharge, soldiers' reading interests shifted dramatically. Demand for technical works and books about the war dropped sharply. About to reenter civilian life and obtain a job, the men looked for information about every imaginable trade and profession. In order to call attention to the vocational literature, reading lists on twenty-three vocational subjects were printed in substantial quantities and prominently displayed in the camps. At the suggestion of the War

Department, a pictorial guide entitled *Your Job Back Home* was prepared and released to the camps. Several dozen occupations were highlighted through excellent photographs and recommended readings. To publicize the camp library as an information center for careers, ''Back to the Job'' placards were posted throughout the camps, and lantern slides were shown in the movie theaters.[63]

By June 30, 1919, thirteen camps libraries had been closed and several months later twenty-five buildings were transferred to the army and navy. Another twelve buildings were sold for an average price of $725. To the consternation of some camp librarians, books from the dismantled camps were not turned over to state library commissions or local libraries. The books were desperately needed in Europe and for hospital libraries.[64]

Although library work in hospitals antedated World War I, the Association's service to hospitalized soldiers surpassed prior accomplishments, and so impressed the federal government that it later assumed financial responsibility for hospital libraries. The Association's hospital work evolved from an adjunct service of the camp library in the fall of 1917 to a major commitment by the summer of 1918. In June 1918, twenty-two ALA librarians were serving in military hospital libraries. Hospital work expanded rapidly in 1919 after the U.S. Public Health Service opened special treatment centers, known as reconstruction hospitals, for discharged soldiers. By the spring of 1919 there were sixty-eight hospital librarians and thirty-six assistants serving in military and reconstruction hospitals. In addition to the 68 hospitals with resident ALA librarians, another 160 hospitals received ALA books and magazines.[65]

Plans for a systematic ALA hospital service date from the appointment of Caroline F. Webster of the New York State Library to the Washington staff on February 15, 1918. For the duration of the war and beyond, she served as the chief of the ALA's hospital library service. Webster's first task was to query the army and navy concerning the number of hospitals and their size. Government departments and the Red Cross offered full cooperation, but local medical commanders, unfamiliar with the benefits of library service, were less receptive. All of them wanted books, but some were cool to the idea of a resident librarian. Admiration soon replaced the skepticism of at least one army medical commander. After the ALA librarian completed her tour, the commander wired this terse request to war service headquarters: ''Competent librarian needed and demanded.''[66]

Field representatives assisted Caroline Webster in the management of the hospital libraries. The representatives—Miriam E. Carey, Minnesota State Board of Control; Caroline L. Jones, Carnegie Library of Pittsburgh; Edith K. Jones, McLean Hospital; Ernestine Rose, Carnegie Library School; and Ola M. Wyeth, University of Illinois Library—made impressive contributions to the overall success of the Association's hospital work. Unlike camp librarians, hospital librarians divided their allegiance between several agencies. At bases with an ALA library, the hospital library was considered a branch of the camp library. The hospital librarian coordinated book orders and other matters with the camp librarian, but was ultimately responsible to hospital officials. In hospitals where there was no camp library, the hospital librarian communicated directly with the Washington staff, but again reported to local medical officers or Red Cross supervisors.[67]

The effectiveness of the hospital library service was enhanced by the cooperation of public libraries and the Red Cross. Public libraries frequently sent books and magazines to hospitals in their areas and sometimes donated members of their staff to organize collections in those hospitals without a librarian. When the Red Cross decided to establish convalescent houses in the camps, one of its first actions was to invite the ALA to extend library service to the new facilities. Ninety-two convalescent houses were built by February 1919. By that time, too, the Red Cross had distributed 60,000 books, just over 4,000 magazines, and nearly 15,000 scrapbooks within the camps.[68]

Although the Association's relations with the Red Cross leadership were generally excellent, some friction was evident. Elizabeth Pomeroy, formerly with the Michigan State Library, complained to Caroline Webster in May 1919 that the Red Cross field director at the U.S. Army hospital in Detroit was uncooperative. Newspapers delivered to the hospital were not being distributed to the patients. Adam Strohm of the Detroit Public Library corroborated Pomeroy's sense of anguish over the incident: "I am hopelessly disgusted with the frequent exploitation of individual workers. The spirit of the service, namely that of giving, is unknown to them but an opportunity to advertise and enhance themselves and their petty vanity is never neglected."[69]

Hospital library collections were small in comparison to those in the camp libraries. Collections in hospitals without an ALA librarian probably averaged 1,000 volumes. Larger collections of between 3,000 and 5,000 volumes were available in the hospitals served by a resident librarian. Approximately twenty periodicals were provided to each hospital.[70] Considering the small size of these libraries and hospital populations of no more than 2,000 patients and staff, circulation rates were very high. The U.S. Public Health Hospital at Fort Bayard, New Mexico, reported an average monthly circulation of 2,092 volumes during the period June 1920-May 1921.[71] Fiction invariably circulated more frequently than nonfiction, usually by a margin of better than three-to-one.

The most popular services of the hospital library were the daily distribution of home town newspapers and the librarians's personal visit with the book wagon to the bedridden patients. Even with three or four assistants, the librarian could manage only a weekly visit to the wards in the larger hospitals. Older books, paperbacks, and magazines were also sent to the contagious wards and burned after the patients read them. The library collections were a vital component of the vocational rehabilitation programs in many hospitals. Modest reference collections were maintained in major hospitals for the benefit of the medical staff.[72]

Ministering to the library needs of disabled veterans was a dedicated calling. Edith Jones recalled the grim conditions and depressing atmosphere faced by many hospital librarians. If the conditions were sometimes disheartening, the rewards associated with hospital work sustained the librarians. The soldiers were always happy to see their "booklady." Through close personal contact, hospital librarians came to know their clients as few librarians did. Whether helping an illiterate patient to read or relieving the tedium with an upbeat novel, hospital librarians usually visited with their patients more than once. Observing the soldiers recuperating and believing that their progress was due, in part, to reading was an intensely satisfying experience for the hospital librarians.[73]

Hospital librarians held an abiding, almost evangelical faith in the curative power of controlled reading. That faith in reading as a therapeutic agent gained many converts during and after the war. Bibliotherapy came of age during World War I, a direct consequence of the Association's library service in hospitals. Articles by hospital librarians proliferated in the 1920s, extolling the virtues of hospital libraries in the medical and nursing literature. State library commissions, public libraries, and private hospitals reexamined their views regarding hospital library service.[74] After seeing the beneficial effects of hospital library service in the camp where he served as librarian, Clarence Sumner of the Sioux City (Iowa) Public Library instituted library service in each of the city's six hospitals in 1919.[75]

FOUR

'Over There':
Service in Europe

Extension of the Association's war work to Europe and other foreign locations in the spring of 1918 introduced new problems and created new opportunities. For a number of months, the transportation of library materials to England and France became a logistical nightmare. Distributing books to the mobile soldiers in the AEF was far more difficult than dispensing books to the soldiers in fixed locations in the United States. And at times, relations between the Association and the YMCA were more fractious in Europe than in the United States.

The selection of McKendree L. Raney to supervise the ALA's overseas library operations was a felicitous one, a choice which Herbert Putnam never regretted. A Johns Hopkins Ph.D. and director of its library since 1908, Raney possessed the right attributes for a tough assignment. By nature forthright and decisive, Raney was an able administrator; and, as his sensitive dealings with the YMCA demonstrate, he was obviously a skilled negotiator. He needed to summon all of these resources to review library conditions in Europe and to chart a course of action for the Association.

Bearing letters of introduction from the secretaries of war and navy, Raney sailed for London aboard the U.S.S. *St. Louis* on January 20, 1918. For several weeks Raney conferred with officials of the British government, the Red Cross, and the YMCA. The two welfare agencies were well established in England, where their library departments supplied books to the Allied soldiers. Raney found that library service to the troops in England, including the American contingent, was generally satisfactory.

There was little hope, then, for a merger between the Association and the other welfare groups. These agencies had perfected their staffs and programs to the point where shared authority, as distinct from informal cooperation, would be considered an intrusion. The only sound course, Raney believed, was to "throw resources into the scales to tip the beam in favor of a creditable, distinctive service for the A.L.A."[1] Books for the American soldiers in Europe must come from the United States. Only American books would satisfy our soldiers, Raney was told by the troops already fighting in Europe. Officials of the YMCA advised Raney to steer clear of the British book market. Three years of gift solicitations and purchases by the various British agencies had depleted the country's book supply, especially in London.

Arriving in Paris on February 13, Raney began a round of talks with the welfare agencies and military authorities. These discussions reinforced his initial belief that the Association must pursue an independent course. Only one man in France could grant exclusive jurisdiction over library service to the Association—General John J. Pershing, Commander of the American Expeditionary Force.

Raney outlined the Association's needs and future plans to Pershing on February 20. Although exclusive status for the ALA was highly desirable in order to prevent duplication among the welfare agencies, the Association expected to cooperate with the YMCA and Red Cross and to use their facilities as distribution points. An ALA representative would be sent to France to coordinate library affairs. Raney also requested authorization to ship fifty tons of books (approximately 75,000 volumes) per month. The Association wanted nothing for itself, Raney told Pershing, only the opportunity for altruistic service. Impressed by Raney's approach, Pershing personally commended him the next day for an "excellent statement" and a "commendable plan." Raney's propposal was promptly approved by Pershing and the tonnage request sent to Washington.[2]

In contrast to the smooth operations in England, the YMCA's Library Bureau in Paris badly needed a thorough housecleaning. Few books had been dispatched to the soldiers' huts, no trained librarians were in the field, and future plans were nonexistent. Raney had little difficulty isolating the main cause of the bureau's ineffectiveness. Since late 1917, the man in charge had been Walter Briggs, assistant librarian of the Harvard College Library. On the basis of several brief talks with a member of the Library War Council and ALA President Thomas L. Montgomery, the misguided Briggs went to Europe for the purpose of representing the YMCA as well as the Association.[3]

Raney liked Briggs personally, but evidence of Briggs' incompetence was abundant. When Raney asked Briggs to produce the documents authorizing him to act on behalf of the Association, none were submitted. Diplomatically but firmly, Raney then pressed YMCA officials to reorganize the library bureau and to dismiss Briggs. With the sympathetic concurrence of Edward C. Carter, the YMCA's chief officer in France, and Dr. Anson Phelps Stokes, secretary of Yale University and the YMCA's educational adviser, the library bureau was realigned. Sidney Morse became the nominal head of the bureau while Briggs was quietly exiled to another post. Burton E. Stevenson, who arrived in France on April 13 to serve as the ALA's European representative, reported to Raney several weeks later that he had seen Briggs "still wandering about the town like a sheeted ghost."[4]

Stevenson, too, quickly perceived the YMCA's willingness to accept credit for the ALA's library service. After reading the draft of a YMCA circular which announced that the Association would pass title to the books it delivered to cooperating agencies, Stevenson was troubled by the lack of proper credit. Pointedly, Stevenson told Morse that the Association did not pass title to other organizations; rather, it retained a "trusteeship" over the books given by the American people.[5] In a report to Herbert Putnam about the incident, Stevenson predicted a bitter struggle with the YMCA culminating in a "war to the knife."[6]

As the YMCA became aware of the Association's intention—and ability—to set library policy in Europe, its attitude shifted from indifference to wary cooperation. Raney understood from the outset that the ALA was much more dependent upon the YMCA in Europe than in America, where the camp libraries were visible evidence of the Association's independent status. By contrast, the European facilities of the YMCA would be indispensable outlets for ALA books and magazines. Adroitly appealing to the YMCA's self-interest, Raney worked to rebuild its library department. At the same time, he resisted attempts by the YMCA to assimilate the ALA program, thereby firmly establishing the Association's primacy over library affairs in Europe.

Developing a constructive relationship with the Red Cross was much easier than with the YMCA. Raney travelled to Brest in March to inspect three naval bases and, secondarily, to meet with Admiral Henry B. Wilson, Commander of U.S. Naval Forces in France. Admiral Wilson was especially pleased that one of the welfare groups had taken an interest in the navy. All of the attention was being lavished on the army, he said. The admiral promptly invited Raney to join the fleet at sea. For two days Raney had the run of the admiral's ship, talking with the officers and men about their reading habits and library needs. The navy provided amply stocked libraries for its battleships and other large vessels, but the smaller ships and naval aviation bases needed library materials. As soon as he returned, Raney ordered 8,000 books for the navy men in Brest, Bordeaux, and St. Nazaire.[7]

Before leaving France in May, Raney scheduled a conference with General Pershing's staff liaison for welfare organizations. Once the ALA books arrived in quantity and were distributed to field units, Raney feared that the books might be mistreated. He proposed that the proper care of library materials be made the subject of an army general order. The staff liaison demurred; placing the books under military custody would alienate the men. A compromise was effected whereby a motto, signed by General Pershing, would appear on placards in the ALA libraries and on the bookplate of each volume. Raney's suggested slogan was approved by Pershing:

These books come to us overseas from home;
To read them is a privilege;
To restore them promptly unabused a duty.[8]

After Raney's departure, Stevenson further consolidated the Association's position and devised procedures for distributing library materials. Four subjects demanded most of Stevenson's attention from April 1918 to the fall of that year: refining relations with the YMCA; monitoring the shipments of books from the United States; establishing a central library in Paris; and developing a network of regional libraries to serve the AEF.

Although Raney had attempted to improve rapport between the ALA and YMCA library representatives, Stevenson reported continuing obstructions. According to Stevenson, Sidney Morse of the YMCA library section was turning his office into a "nest of intrigue" and making a "general nuisance" of himself. Stevenson caught Morse stealing some ALA correspondence and reported the incident to Morse's superior, Dr. John Erskine, chief of the YMCA's educational department. Morse was soon transferred. The cumulative effect of Raney's and Stevenson's encounters with the YMCA led to a curious interorganizational relationship. By the summer of 1918, Stevenson was exercising *de facto* control over the YMCA's library activities.[9]

Another irritant was the YMCA's frequent use of a deposit system for its books, a practice which required each soldier to pay a sum in advance for circulation privileges. From the inception of its military library service, the Association had circulated books under an honor code without fees. By June 1918, Stevenson convinced the YMCA that deposits were interpreted by many soldiers as a rationale for not returning books. Furthermore, the Association would not tolerate a fee arrangement for ALA books. The YMCA grudgingly consented, although some field secretaries continued to impose fees throughout the war.[10]

Shipping books and magazines from America to Europe was a difficult logistical task. The first shipment, presumably addressed to YMCA officials in England and France, left the New York dispatch office prior to December 1, 1917. Shipments started from the Hoboken dispatch office in January 1918, and by May the six overseas dispatch offices were sending over 100,000 volumes a month. Stevenson received the first shipment of several thousand volumes in April 1918. Of the slightly more than 2.5 million volumes sent to Europe, approximately 1.3 million arrived before the Armistice. The monthly cargo allotment of fifty tons proved inadequate. Additional space was obtained by deck shipments, utilizing the tonnage allocations of the YMCA and Red Cross.[11]

Approximately 40 percent of these shipments never reached France. About 1.5 million volumes were actually received. There were numerous reasons for the drastic losses enroute. Early shipments were occasionally mislabelled and vanished from ALA custody. Several ships carrying Association books were torpedoed and sunk. Such losses were minimal compared to those resulting from the practice of permitting the men leaving the United States to take books aboard and then deposit them with the YMCA after arriving in France. Another practice, which allowed book cases aboard ship to be opened during the voyage and then repacked, also contributed to the heavy losses.[12]

Raney initially suspected the YMCA transport secretaries, but eventually traced the losses to a "monumental blunder" by the Association.[13] During January 1918, Herbert Putnam had requested and received permission from the military authorities to allow the men to carry books overseas. He then notified dispatch offices and camp libraries that soldiers could take books aboard the transport ships and deposit them with the nearest YMCA facility upon disembarkation. Frederick Pottle, the future literary scholar, was among those who were delighted to tuck away several ALA books before leaving Camp Merritt (New Jersey). Putnam's naive plan, conceived for the soldiers' benefit, was often abused. Many books were kept by the soldiers. Raney, in an effort to minimize losses, persuaded the army to supervise the opening and repacking of deck shipments.[14]

Other welfare organizations also distributed reading materials to the AEF. Each of the commission agencies distributed magazines, religious publications, and general purpose books. In England, the

YMCA distributed 1.8 million items and shipments to France totalled 5,000,000 items. Of this figure, 1.4 million were general books and 327,837 were texts.[15] Although the YMCA distributed nearly as many general books as the Association, several distinctions regarding the library service of the two agencies are important: collections assembled by the Association were generally more diversified and contained fewer multiple copies than the YMCA collections; substantial numbers of YMCA books were sold to the troops while all ALA books were free; and one-third or more of the YMCA's fifty-eight librarians were released or detailed to the Association.[16] Most YMCA hut libraries were under the supervision of educational secretaries who had little or no library experience. In the YMCA huts where YMCA and ALA books commingled, the entire collection was subject, in theory at least, to Association policies.

While the fighting continued, and the number of ALA librarians allowed in France was restricted to a minimum, the Association made extensive use of library personnel from the YMCA and the Red Cross. Following the Armistice, however, additional ALA librarians came from the United States and trained library workers in the army became available. By May 1920, ninety librarians had served with the Association. Of that total, sixty-three were women and twenty-seven were men. Twenty of the ninety librarians were transferred from the YMCA and five were released by the Red Cross. The payroll was swelled by another 100 employees who served in supportive capacities.[17]

The librarians, many of whom were former camp librarians or dispatch office managers, were personally selected by Stevenson. Librarians serving in Europe were seasoned professionals, and included Samuel H. Ranck, Grand Rapids (Michigan) Public Library; Judson T. Jennings, Seattle Public Library; Mary F. Isom, Portland (Oregon) Public Library; Willis H. Kerr, Kansas State Normal School Library; Luther L. Dickerson, Grinnell College Library; Harry O. Severance, University of Missouri Library; Harriet C. Long, Van Wert (Ohio) Public Library; and Rudolph H. Gjelsness, University of Illinois Library School. For seven months beginning in January 1919, Herbert Putnam and his daughter Shirley resided at the Association's headquarters in Paris.[18]

From the beginning, said Stevenson, the ALA wanted to do "far more than dump a miscellaneous lot of books in France."[19] Furnishing the appropriate books needed by the soldiers was the professional ideal which guided Stevenson's approach to distributing reading material and staffing libraries. Books arrived from the United States in cases (designed by Joseph L. Wheeler) which allowed for almost instant library service. Books were packed in specially constructed cases with a central shelf; when stacked the cases formed a sectional book case. Every book was supplied with a charge card. Placards and circulars of information were enclosed in the cases to explain circulation and return procedures.[20]

The AEF was dispersed throughout France, divided between relatively stable rear areas and constantly shifting battle lines. In order to reach as many soldiers as possible, Stevenson utilized three main points of contact: welfare organizations, military units, and ALA-operated regional libraries. By spring, 1919, book collections varying in size from 100 to 6,000 volumes had been placed in 636 YMCA huts, 41 Salvation Army cabins, 55 Knights of Columbus huts, 17 YMCA hostess houses, 7 centers of the Jewish Welfare Board, and 35 Foyers du Soldat (French YMCA). Distrustful of the YMCA to the end, Stevenson preferred to distribute books directly to the military units. Slightly more than 700 field units received portable libraries. Before these collections were dispersed, military units agreed to place the materials under adequate supervision.[21]

Because of transportation and distribution problems, it soon became apparent that additional library centers were needed. These centers, or regional libraries, were set up in strategic locations to serve troops stationed in the immediate area and to function as distribution points for the adjoining areas. Through an arrangement with the YMCA, most of the regional libraries were staffed by YMCA personnel released to the Association and housed in YMCA facilities. Eleven of these centers were maintained at such locations as Chaumont, Dijon, Marseille, Nantes, and Châttilon-sur-Seine. Eight more regional centers, in buildings devoted exclusively to library service, were opened starting in January 1919. Supervised by ALA librarians, these centers were established in Beaune, Brest, Coblenz, Gièvres, Le Mans, St. Aignan, St. Nazaire, and Savenay. Library collections at these regional centers averaged 30,000 to 50,000 volumes.[22]

Development of the overseas library service, from initial organization to operational maturity, consumed about eight months. This experience coincided with the amount of time needed to create a viable camp library system in the United States. By summer, 1918, the Association's European library program was receiving compliments and support from military officials and the Commission on Training Camp Activities. General Pershing, courted by Stevenson with considerable success, told the European representative that AEF assistance and resources would be "cheerfully put at the disposal of the American Library Association.''[23] After visiting France, Raymond Fosdick was very pleased with the ALA's progress and transmitted this flattering appraisal to Herbert Putnam:

> I found your books everywhere, from the seaport bases to the front line trenches. I found them in dugouts thirty to forty feet below the ground, in cow-barns where the shrapnel had blown part of the roof away, as well as in substantial huts and tents far back from the firing line. And they were well worn books that I saw, showing signs of constant usage. Indeed, the books are in continual demand, I am sure that it will be a reading army that we shall welcome home. . . .[24]

Since his arrival in France, Stevenson had conducted business from the Hotel de Crillon and later from a rented office in the YMCA's administrative building at No. 12, rue d'Aguesseau. As the Association's library work expanded, more suitable quarters were needed to accommodate the supervisory staff and to house a central reference collection. Initially, Stevenson agreed with Raney about a shared facility with the Red Cross, but an invitation from the YMCA to join them in new quarters at No. 10 rue de l'Elysée was too enticing to resist. When Stevenson learned that Red Cross officials intended to control any future library in their quarters, he speedily accepted the YMCA offer, and moved in on July 30.[25] The new arrangement would be most beneficial, Stevenson confided to Herbert Putnam, because it ''permits us to impose our authority and to display our resources in an exceptional manner.''[26]

''I dare say no public library was ever before installed amid such glittering surroundings,'' Stevenson reminisced after the war. Located on a stately residential street running alongside the Palais de l'Elysée, the building had been the residence of the Papal Nuncio to the French Republic. Great mirrors rose to the ceiling above marble mantles; cherubs adorned gilt cornices which encircled every room; the floors were of elegant parquetry; tapestried silk and satin lined the walls; and a striking marble staircase connected the floors.[27] ''An enchanted palace,'' one of the librarians called the building—and full of pleasant surprises: just when the library needed more storage space, someone would stumble upon a secret passage or a concealed stairway.[28]

In this sumptuous residence Stevenson could pursue an idea which had been germinating for several months. He had already been laying aside one copy of each technical work arriving from America to form the nucleus of a centralized reference library. The library would serve several purposes, Stevenson informed General Pershing. Foreshadowing a books-by-mail program, Stevenson wanted to acquire an extensive collection of technical books which could be supplied to soldiers in the field. Another objective involved using the library as a "living demonstration" in France of the American public library. Such an American model, Stevenson believed, might be adopted in France after the war. Finally, the library would not only be available to the AEF, but also to the English speaking residents of France.[29]

The Paris Library opened on August 29, 1918, following a hectic month during which 7,000 volumes were cataloged and shelved. Staff members, who worked indefatigably to get the library ready, included Mrs. Burton Stevenson; Mary J. Booth, Illinois State Normal School Library; Mrs. Frederick Palmer, wife of the famous war correspondent; and Elizabeth G. Potter, Oakland (California) Public Library. Within a year the library had amassed a collection of approximately 15,000 volumes. Primarily intended for the serious reader, the library's holdings were particularly strong in subjects pertaining to American history, economics, sociology, and technology. Even with the city of Paris and the library shrouded in darkness to avert air raids, it did not take long for the soldiers to discover the place where American books and magazines were available. Open seven days a week, the library did a brisk business, circulating about 4,500 volumes per month.[30]

Three distinct phases of reader interest were reported. Technical literature was called for most often while the war was in progress. Then fiction predominated for the several restless months following the Armistice. Finally, the library entered an educational phase in the spring of 1919 when the men studied cultural subjects or updated their knowledge about various vocational specialties. Nearly all of the AEF soldiers attending the Sorbonne found their way to the library. The various postwar commissions sent to such countries as Poland and Armenia regularly used the library's extensive collection of social science materials.

Realizing that library service at the established posts would never reach all of the soldiers, Stevenson initiated plans, in August 1918, for a books-by-mail program. General Pershing granted franking privileges to the Association within a month. Books could be sent through the army postal system to military units and to individual soldiers. Using the mails to send books to areas without regular library services was not a new idea; mailing books had been proposed before the turn of the century. Certainly, however, the practice of mailing books directly to patrons was not widespread before Stevenson's operation.[31]

No service proved more popular with the AEF soldiers than the books-by-mail program. Several advertisements were run in *Stars and Stripes,* the AEF newspaper, informing the men that books could be

McKendree Raney

Burton E. Stevenson

ordered from the Paris Library and from the ALA library in Coblenz. Each soldier unable to visit a library in the field was entitled to two books which he could retain for a month. As word spread of the new service, the Paris Library was deluged with requests. Mrs. Stevenson, who supervised the mailing department, started with a staff of two persons in September 1918. Three months later the department had been expanded to include five librarians and twelve clerks and typists.[32] Between January and July 1919, the mailing department circulated 32,012 books to individual soldiers and probably four times that number in bulk mailings to military units. Applications sometimes exceeded 2,000 per day. Nine out of ten soldiers asked for nonfiction. At first, many orders could not be filled, but as the supply of books was augmented the fill-rate improved to about 90 percent. The books were returned with commendable promptness and losses were minimal.[33]

Aware of the value of effective publicity, Stevenson appointed the redoubtable Mary E. Ahern as publicity coordinator for the overseas Library War Service. Books were still needed after the Armistice, and Stevenson believed that the European library work would not be covered adequately in the press without generating publicity materials from the Paris headquarters. From January to June 1919, Ahern furnished articles and editorial copy to a dozen or more periodicals and newspapers. Her complimentary accounts of overseas library activities appeared in such publications as the *Chicago Daily News,* the *Christian Science Monitor, Collier's Weekly,* and *Outlook.*[34]

Outside of Paris, library conditions were quite different. Base Section No. 1 was a sprawling military installation of fifty army and navy camps in northwestern France which encompassed five departments (formerly the province of Brittany). St. Nazaire, at the center of this complex, was a port city on the Loire. The city's prewar population of 38,000 was inflated threefold by the encampment of American soldiers. There were no taxicabs, street cars, or daily newspapers. As the great supply center for the AEF, St. Nazaire had a large contingent of men, many of them black, in the Service of Supply.[35]

Samual H. Ranck, formerly at Camp Custer (Michigan), arrived in St. Nazaire on January 5, 1919, and stayed for nine months. His job at Base Section No. 1, as he soon discovered, was quite unlike the work of a camp librarian in the United States. Satisfying the reading needs of the men was, of course, a common goal; but the conditions—incessant rain, strange customs, a foreign language, and homesick soldiers—made the assignment altogether different. His duties fell under five headings: unloading incoming books from the ships and sending them to Paris; supplying books to soldiers in the region's camps; supporting the instructional work in the camps; furnishing books to naval vessels which did not get back to America for long periods; and salvaging books from military outfits about to return home.

Unloading and forwarding the books to Paris and elsewhere was never a routine activity. On one occasion a YMCA secretary connived with dock officials to use the ALA's shipping allocation as a means of getting his personal belongings to Paris. Ranck thwarted the scheme. Another time, ALA educational books were stolen from a train while it was being loaded. The culprit, an army chaplain, was arrested for the robbery some distance from St. Nazaire.[36]

Soldiers in the camps were highly appreciative of the chance to read. "There had been a book hunger the like of which I did not believe possible," Ranck observed. Lines started forming at the hut libraries before breakfast and kept up nearly all day. In light of this terrific demand, Ranck did not believe that the Association should be unduly concerned about book losses. The only question that counted was, "When the boys were hungry for books to read, did they get them?" Ranck did his best, dispensing books to 190 locations within Base Section No. 1.[37]

Approximately 30,000 black soldiers lived and worked at St. Nazaire. At one camp, a YMCA hut served nearly 8,000 black soldiers. With seating for only seventy-five persons, the library section of the hut was filled most of the time. As reported by Ranck, books of a literary character and poetry were more popular with black soldiers than with white soldiers. Esther Johnson, a white YMCA librarian on loan to the Association, had excellent rapport with the black troops. She started many of the illiterates on beginning readers and read aloud to others. Referring to the black soldiers, Ranck commented that ". . . no class or group of readers appreciate the work of the A.L.A. more than they do."[38]

Californian Ona Rounds journeyed to Châtillon-sur-Seine in January 1919. Straddling the banks of the upper Seine, Châtillon was a town of about 6,000 residents in east central France. Brewing, iron production, and agriculture were the main occupations. Although assigned to a smaller geographical area than Ranck's around St. Nazaire, Rounds had a sizable military population to serve. The 30,000 troops encamped at Châtillon and the men in the sixty isolated outposts depended on her for all of their library needs. Châtillon was already overcrowded by the time of her arrival; the prospective library could not be given a prime location. She had to settle for a dingy, second-floor room in the main YMCA building. Undeterred, Rounds recruited several assistants, wired Paris for books, and dressed up the room. Within a week, the library was filled to capacity every day.[39]

The first shipment of books, mostly gift volumes from America, was a keen disappointment. The men grumbled, "Gee, they do love us, don't they," and Rounds "felt ashamed to look at the boys when we found such a collection." Fortunately, later shipments brought more recent and more interesting titles. Nonlibrary amenities were provided, too. The men could dry their clothes, write letters, and even borrow a backpack for a day. An especially endearing quality of the librarian was her evenhanded treatment of officers and enlisted men. Antagonism between the two groups sharpened during demobilization, and the enlisted men appreciated a place where special favors were not granted to the officers.[40]

Disillusionment and restlessness followed the Armistice in Europe. Some soldiers were embittered, many were lonely, and all were eager to return home. As the weeks and months of waiting elapsed, army morale began to crack, desertions increased, and the resentment between officers and enlisted men intensified. Impatient and aimless, the soldiers vented their emotions in doggerel:

> We drove the Kaiser from his throne,
> We drove the Boche beyond the Rhine—
> Lafayette, we've paid our debt,
> For Christ's sake send us home![41]

Channeling the men's energies into constructive pursuits became a priority concern. Sports were introduced as an outlet and a major educational program was initiated by the YMCA with the assistance of the Association.

With its cadre of educational secretaries and network of huts, the YMCA was in a strategic position to organize an educational program for the AEF. Accordingly, on January 18, 1918, Anson Stokes arrived in France to survey conditions and to recommend a plan. Two reports were submitted to General Pershing in February 1918 and approved, in principle, by the end of the month. The first report, never fully implemented, considered educational opportunities during the war. Special emphasis would be given to instruction on war aims, citizenship, and the French language. In his second report, Stokes anticipated the extended demobilization. Post schools were proposed in which common school-level instruction would be offered in basic subjects and vocational skills. Divisional schools would cover a larger geographical area and provide advanced technical instruction. Soldiers with college training might even attend British and French universities. In August 1918, the YMCA Army Educational Commission, chaired by John Erskine of Columbia University, was established on a permanent basis.[42]

Willis H. Kerr, former librarian at Camp Funston (Kansas), was charged with supervising the library component of this massive educational program. Before Kerr's arrival in December 1918, Stevenson had formulated tentative plans for educational library collections. Two types of collections were envisioned. One collection would be comprised of basic reference volumes and the second collection would contain specialized materials to meet local educational requirements. A standardized list of 900 titles, embracing 121 subjects, was prepared to facilitate ordering and shipping.[43]

Each general reference collection, or "ALA Educational Library," held about 400 volumes. Three hundred sixty-one of these sets were sent to approximately 320 divisional and post schools. Special educational collections were assembled and dispatched to fill particular needs. Nearly 300 of these sets were supplied on such subjects as surveying, business administration, child welfare, and labor relations. Kerr reported that the educational libraries "had an appreciable educational and cultural effect, independent of any instruction." Educational collections were also sent to French and British universities, to army hospitals, and to various missions and relief agencies.[44]

The AEF University at Beaune, a small city in the Côte d'Or region, was the capstone of the army's educational program. Operational for only three months (March-June 1919), the school at midterm offered 240 courses to slightly more than 13,000 students. The University was divided into thirteen colleges and governed by a council consisting of Colonel Ira L. Reeves, superintendent; John Erskine, educational director; directors of the colleges; and the ALA librarian, Luther L. Dickerson. Of the nearly 700 faculty members, 80 percent were military personnel.[45]

The Beaune Library was prepared for use in record time. Dickerson arrived on March 6, 1919, and the library opened a week later with a hastily shelved collection of 6,000 books. Within a very short time, the collection exceeded 30,000 volumes. Over 80 percent of the collection was nonfiction. Every effort was made to purchase the most recent titles; very few gift books were accepted. Initially housed in one building, the library was soon enlarged by two additions. The three connected buildings provided accommodations for 1,500 soldiers, twice the seating capacity of the central library of any American university.[46]

The library staff consisted of twenty-six full-time persons, eight of whom were librarians. In addition to Dickerson, the Library War Service furnished three librarians: Pauline Fullerton (New York Public Library); Francis L. D. Goodrich (University of Michigan Library); and Harriet C. Long. Corporal Rudolph Gjelsness, a student on leave from the University of Illinois Library School, assisted for a time, as did several other librarians who were serving in the AEF. Exceptionally busy, the library's average daily circulation approached 1,100 volumes. During the library's brief existence, 88,500 volumes circulated and attendance was estimated at 310,000.[47]

The military's high regard for the Association's contribution at Beaune was unequivocal. Colonel Reeves was generous in his commendation: "There has not been a single thing . . . pertaining to the establishment of the library which has been criticized; on the other hand, there has been the highest praise of the efficiency with which it has been handled."[48] Luther Dickerson summarized the Beaune experience as the "happiest incident" of his varied assignments."[49] No library in the AEF, or in the domestic camps, was so completely integrated with the instructional process as the library at Beaune. The Association's practical exposure to the potentialities of adult education would not be forgotten. The renewed interest in library adult education in the postwar decade was largely promoted by Library War Service librarians.

When American soldiers of the Third Army marched into the Rhineland in December 1918, the Association was not far behind. Headquarters for the occupation force of 200,000 men was established in Coblenz, Germany. Although troop levels dropped steadily, the occupation lasted until February 1923. Determined to serve the AEF throughout Europe, Stevenson asked Judson T. Jennings to represent the ALA at Coblenz. Jennings stayed only a month, January 1919, and was succeeded by Edward E. Ruby (Whitman College Library, Washington) who served until June. For the next three months Luther Dickerson, fresh from Beaune, directed library activities at Coblenz.

Temporary library quarters were found in the grand Festhalle near the center of the city. As in many other locations, the principal tenant was the YMCA. Besides the library wing on the first floor, the Festhalle was admirably suited as a social center. There was a concert hall, several lounge areas, and dining facilities. Perhaps once a month the men scattered among the 250 permanent stations outside of Coblenz would receive a pass to visit the city. Since German hotels, restaurants, and theaters were off limits to the troops, the Festhalle was a popular attraction.[50]

Although the Third Army had been partially supplied with ALA books before moving to Germany, it was unable to bring the books to Coblenz. For this reason, books were desperately needed in Coblenz and in all of the surrounding stations. Books were slow in arriving because the Paris headquarters could barely meet the heavy demand for educational sets elsewhere. According to Ruby, the "shortage of books at Paris rendered us almost helpless during most of the first three months of our work."[51] Eventually, about 200,000 books reached Coblenz.

An elaborate distribution system was devised to serve the Third Army. The Festhalle library was stocked with 10,000 volumes. Considerably more than one-half of the available books were dispatched to the Knights of Columbus, the Red Cross, and the YMCA. Safeguarding the books was a constant problem in the welfare huts. Ruby, like Stevenson, preferred to send books directly to military units. Of the 236 permanent stations in being as of May 1919, the ALA had furnished library materials to 176. The lack of an adequate book supply and the constant shifting of the military units seriously hampered distribution. Many of the isolated posts never received books.[52]

On September 18, 1919, the central library in Coblenz was moved to a former German officers' club on 42 Rizza Strasse. Lack of funds finally necessitated the ALA's withdrawal from Coblenz on December 31, 1920. Just over 33,000 books were transferred to the army and the YMCA agreed to continue the library. The ALA's library program in Coblenz, extending more than two years beyond the Armistice, contrasts sharply with many of the welfare agencies which had curtailed or eliminated their services during that period.[53]

As the soldiers left France in the summer and fall of 1919, Stevenson worried about the future of the Paris Library. A permanent library in Paris would be a living memorial of the overseas Library War Service, a fine example of American library methods, and a center for the promotion of cultural understanding. Stevenson was deeply committed to the idea of continuing the library, but he also recognized the pragmatic considerations. As the beneficiaries of a permanent library, the residents of Paris must be willing to support a plan of financial maintenance. Several discreet inquiries about backing for the library left Stevenson discouraged. If these residents were unwilling to support the library, Stevenson said, "they didn't want it very badly, and it would better be sent home."[54]

Stevenson decided to test public sentiment. A general meeting to take place in the library was announced in the Paris newspapers. On

Wednesday afternoon, October 26, 1919, Stevenson nervously awaited the verdict. His anxieties were quickly dispelled; a large crowd of concerned residents, French and American, filled the library's meeting room. There was a delegation from the American Chamber of Commerce, the American Woman's Club, and the American University Union. Also attending were interested British residents in Paris, French scholars and students, and the distinguished librarian Paul Otlet of Brussels. Plans were approved for a committee on permanent organization to develop a constitution and to solicit funds. Before adjournment, one of the visitors announced a substantial donation. Charles L. Seeger of the U.S. Rubber Company—father of the poet Alan Seeger, who had died in the war—donated the royalties from his son's books. Within several weeks, sufficient funds were obtained to ensure the library's existence for another year.[55]

Many prominent individuals rallied behind the library. Judge Walter Berry, president of the American Chamber of Commerce, agreed to serve as chairman of the general executive committee. Solomon Reinach, eminent archaeologist, accepted the chairmanship of the French committee, and British Vice-Council Hugh London chaired the British committee. Other notables endorsing the library were Raymond Poincaré, former president of the French Republic; Marshal Ferdinand Foch and philosopher Henri Bergson of the French Academy; and expatriate American novelist Edith Wharton.[56]

With only minor reservations, the ALA Executive Board and the War Service Committee, in December 1919, ratified the idea of a permanent institution to be known as the American Library in Paris. As prescribed in the constitution, the Association would have a significant voice in the library's internal affairs; it would reserve authority to appoint the librarian and one-third of the directors. Subsequent modifications of the library's services or quarters had to be cleared with the Executive Board. The American Library in Paris was incorporated under Delaware law in May 1920.[57]

Prospects appeared bright for the new institution. The first director, William N. C. Carlton of the prestigious Newberry Library (Chicago), contemplated a vigorous international role. He wanted to assemble a highly trained staff and adopt the latest American library practices. Future services might include interlibrary loans; exhibitions of American library equipment and new American books; preparation of bibliographies; and training sessions for European librarians.[58]

The dream was only partially realized. A separately funded school for librarians, the Paris Library School, operated from 1923 until 1929 when it fell victim to hard economic times. The ALA Executive Board voted $25,000 for the library's endowment in April 1921, but Library War Service funds were so low the next year that another subvention was not possible.[59] Later, smaller payments were resumed. Subscriber fees, private donations, and grants from philanthropic foundations kept the library afloat, but these funds were barely adequate for a program of international library extension. The goal that the library would become a citadel of American culture for teachers and researchers failed to materialize. When Stevenson returned to France in 1925 to direct the library for five years, he found little call for nonfiction. Fiction constituted almost 70 percent of the total circulation in 1929. "I had the uneasy feeling that we were selling our birthright for a mess of pottage," lamented Stevenson.[60]

FIVE

Celebration, Decline, and Termination

A self-congratulatory mood pervaded the Association's first post-war conference, held at Asbury Park, New Jersey, in June 1919. Descriptions and appraisals of the recent war work dominated the five-day meeting. Of the fifty-one papers delivered at the conference, no fewer than twenty-seven related to various aspects of the Library War Service.

Understandably elated over the success of its war program, the ALA also faced critical choices about the future. Should the wartime activities quietly run their course and expire? If not, what arrangements could be made with the military authorities and other government agencies to continue the library service on a permanent basis? And equally as important, what peacetime goals and programs should be pursued and how would they be financed?

In the early phase of the war work, recalled incoming ALA President Chalmers Hadley, the Association suffered from a lack of public recognition. At one time or another the ALA had been referred to as the American Laundry Association and even the Australian Light Artillery. Gradually, that casual image was replaced by a general recognition of the Association's mission and contributions. Unsolicited commendations from soldiers, senior military officials, and private citizens confirmed what librarians wanted to hear: the Association had reached a new level of acceptance. Hadley said special credit should be given to the many young library workers, who did such a fine job in the camps and hospitals. He believed that female librarians in particular had overcome their prudish image. Perhaps the war's most important lesson for the future was the imaginative and effective use of publicity.[1]

While prideful reminiscence was in order, conceded ALA President William Warner Bishop, the future must also command the organization's attention. The Association was at the "crossroads," Bishop asserted; there could be no return to the *status quo ante*. The great library pioneers of 1876 were nearly all gone and the second generation was approaching retirement. With the help of the young librarians who performed so well in the Library War Service, the Association should "strike out into new fields."[2] Herbert Putnam, still in France, corroborated Bishop's view: "The American Library Association has emerged from an organization with aims supposedly purely professional, into a public service organization."[3]

A special feature of the Asbury conference was the daily appearance of a lively ten-page newspaper, *The Use of Print*. Promoted and edited by Lloyd W. Josselyn, the paper carried extracts of convention speeches, editorials, and advertisements. Available without charge to conferees, the newspaper was also mailed to 7,000 libraries in the United States and Canada, and to over 350 newspapers and periodicals. And it was through this source that members read a sweeping attack of the wartime program.

To John Cotton Dana, the self-indulgent congratulations at Asbury were narcissistic and unwarranted. He believed that the government grossly underestimated the educational and library needs of the military forces, and that the Association, a small voluntary group of librarians, was naive to tender its services without a corresponding promise of massive federal aid.[4] Adding a visual fillip to his argument, Dana passed out copies of a cartoon which he had commissioned for the conference. This humorous sketch depicted an ALA member staring into a mirror while donning a laurel crown inscribed with the words, "For War Work, With Love."[5] Dana properly lanced the proposition that the Library War Service was an unqualified success, but he evaded the central question. If the Association had requested substantial government aid and it had been rebuffed, should the opportunity have been bypassed? But the membership, flushed with pride over its recent accomplishments, was hardly in the mood for Dana's sobering retrospection.

The testimonials at Asbury Park were but a euphoric interlude in the fast-moving thrust of events. Responding to new conditions of the postwar period, a special publicity campaign was activated; vocational publications were rushed into print; certain wartime services were continued; and surplus books were distributed. The War Service Committee presided over the diminishing war work until its dissolution in June 1920. After that date, Library War Service funds were administered by the Executive Board. A special committee, the Committee on the Transfer of Library War Service Activities, was appointed to advise the Executive Board.

Throughout most of 1919 Carl Milam served as acting general director of the Library War Service. While Putnam was in Europe, Milam had full responsibility for the domestic portion of the program. Milam's capacity for hard work and his administrative skills impressed peers and superiors alike. Putnam decided to resign from the Library War Service, effective December 1919; and the thirty-five year old Milam was elevated to the general director's post on December 13. Putnam resumed his duties at the Library of Congress, and the Library War Service staff was transferred to New York City. This smooth transition enabled the final phase of the war work to proceed without loss of momentum.

There were several reasons for continuing publicity after the war. The dominant motive was an altruistic concern for the returning soldiers. Library War Service officials shifted their attention to the public library as the logical agency to alleviate the ex-servicemen's readjustment problems. As a result of this decision, former servicemen were encouraged to depend upon local public libraries as sources of current information on the trades and professions. Stimulation of public support for the extension of library services to unserved areas, especially in rural communities, was a subsidiary motive of the postwar publicity.[6]

Three major bibliographies covering technical, business, and general subjects were issued.[7] A paper edition of *Your Job Back Home,* entitled *The Job Book,* was printed for distribution by a newspaper advertising agency. Over 35,000 copies were distributed to international unions affiliated with the American Federation of Labor. One hundred thousand copies of a poster, ''Knowledge Wins,'' were sent to business schools, labor unions, magazines, and public libraries. Lantern slides for use in movie theaters were made available to public libraries. Articles portraying the Association's wartime accomplishments were commissioned for educational journals, and various ALA leaders spoke at state meetings of the National Educational Association. One publication was unabashedly promotional, obviously designed to impress the general public as well as special interest groups. *Books at War,* a pictorial review of the Association's activities, was furnished to libraries, educational institutions, and selected periodicals.[8]

The U.S. Bureau of Education printed and disseminated a special series of home study courses, known as ''After War Reading Courses,'' in 1919. Under the editorial supervision of Joseph L. Wheeler, twenty of these extension courses were prepared on a variety of civic, literary, historical, and technical subjects. Among the course titles were "Heroes of American Democracy," "Thirty Books of Great Fiction," and "Machine Shop Work." Each course of study included a list of ten to twenty recommended titles. After 1921, the courses were prepared by the bureau until the series was discontinued in 1927. Nearly 30,000 persons enrolled in the courses, and between 2,000 and 3,000 of those registered received certificates of completion.[9]

The Association maintained a number of war-related library services during the years 1919-1921. Just before the Armistice, the War Service Committee agreed to supply books to munitions factories and other war industries. Service was available to thirty plants in locations where library commissions or local public libraries could not provide adequate support. This project was phased out in late 1920. Two other services commenced after the war when the ALA sent library materials to 325 stations of the U.S. Coast Guard and to 724 lighthouses.[10] Both services were transferred to their respective government agencies in 1920.

Library service to the U.S. Navy and to other government shipping agencies assumed major proportions during the war. Approximately 300 naval bases and thousands of vessels were supplied with books and magazines. Over 300,000 books were placed on 150 government transports for the soldiers returning from France in 1919.[11] In July 1919, service was extended to ships of the United States Shipping Board, a government agency created in 1916. U.S.S.B. ships were freight-carriers manned by civilian crews. By December 1919, the Association was serving all merchant ships flying the American flag. When service was terminated to merchant ships on November 30, 1920, nearly 500,000 books had been placed on 2,892 different vessels.[12]

Despite persistent efforts by the Association, no government agency or private seamen's group was prepared to accept responsibility for continuing library service to merchant ships. During the war, Alice Sturtevant Howard administered a social service bureau within the United States Shipping Board. Afterward, she remained a zealous advocate of seamen's welfare. Howard appeared before the Executive Board and the War Service Committee several times during 1920-1921 to plead the value of merchant marine libraries and to forestall the impending termination of that service. She received much sympathy, but no aid.[13] Finally, Howard decided in May 1920 to form an independent organization, the American Merchant Marine Library Association. She served as the first president. As an indication of its support, the ALA transferred about 65,000 volumes and $5,000 in unexpended funds to the new association. Four years later, the American Merchant Marine Library Association had opened a dozen dispatch offices and reported an aggregate circulation of 224,808 for the merchant fleet.[14]

Of the injuries suffered by men in war, perhaps none evoked more compassion than the plight of blinded soldiers. Learning of an acute shortage of braille books for these soldiers, the Association allocated funds to produce additional titles. Gertrude T. Rider, chief of the Blind Division at the Library of Congress and chairman of the ALA's Committee on Work with the Blind, was chosen to supervise the program. She established close relations with the Red Cross Institute for the Blind and with other concerned agencies.[15]

Authors were asked to defray part of the cost of producing braille copies. Donations covered the expense of embossing the text on metal plates. The Association paid for printing, binding, and distribution. Very few authors declined to participate. Among those authors consenting to underwrite the printing of their books were Albert Payson Terhune, Zane Grey, Ida Tarbell, and Edith Wharton.[16] Fifty titles were prepared for blind soldiers and civilians after this project was merged with the Enlarged Program in 1920. Deeply appreciative of the ALA's commitment to the blind, Helen Keller responded movingly:

> Surely the joy and interest which books bring to sightless people who live barren lives is the strongest plea for the work of the American Library Association. . . . Perhaps the worst thing about blindness is, it makes us feel apart from the ways of our fellow men. Books charm away bitterness, and lo, the fulness of life is ours![17]

Long before these postwar activities were discontinued, there were numerous requests for surplus ALA books from libraries and social welfare groups. Anticipating the eventual distribution of these books, the War Service Committee approved a plan in April 1919 which set criteria for their release. Surplus books would be given to state library commissions after meeting the ALA's primary obligation to the soldiers. Following the transfer of large quantities of books to the military services, about 300,000 volumes were declared surplus. Starting in January 1920, the books were shipped to state library agencies in proportion to the number of men from each state in service during the war. These agencies, in turn, sent the books to needy libraries and to public service organizations.[18]

The Association's library service for the army and navy could not continue indefinitely after the Armistice. Officials of the United War Work Campaign decided in November 1918 that funds from this cam-

"Knowledge Wins"—United War Work Campaign Poster

"For War Work, With Love"—Cartoon by Louis Wisa

paign could not be expended for permanent installations or for endowments. Since nearly all of the War Service Committee's budget consisted of these funds, the Association was hardly in a position to support permanent services. Even without this fiscal barrier, the War Service Committee was not inclined to prolong the army and navy service beyond 1919. Unlike the other six agencies of the Commission on Training Camp Activities, the Association was a professional body which saw itself as having been "invited to render a particular professional service during a particular emergency."[19] Its wartime program either had to be phased out or assimilated by the military.

Rather than let the camp library service expire, the War Service Committee decided to pursue an orderly transfer of this service to the military departments. The committee sent letters to the army and navy on January 30, 1919, expressing its desire to arrange a mutually acceptable plan for permanent military library service. If satisfactory terms could be negotiated, the Association was willing to transfer books, buildings, and personnel. Acceptable terms were never really in doubt, but troublesome differences of opinion over the status of librarians surfaced.[20]

On being informed that the navy's new Morale Division might place librarians under the supervision of chaplains, Carl Milam took vigorous exception. "This will never work," he complained.[21] Chaplains had traditionally been responsible for station libraries and their stewardship of these collections had often been less than enlightened. Milam wanted greater recognition for librarians; they should be responsible to station morale officers. The navy, however, would promise only that chaplains would not actually perform as librarians. Chaplains would, however, occasionally supervise professional librarians.[22]

Milam, in conducting most of the negotiations pertaining to the transfer, emphasized the need for a professional library service in the military. The army, he hoped, would provide a trained librarian in every camp, furnish a generous supply of books, and allocate enough money for the preparation of reading lists and publicity activities.[23] Milam wanted the navy to assign librarians to large stations and at least one librarian to the fleet. Captain (Chaplain) J. F. B. Carruthers, chief of the navy's Morale Division, was impressed by Milam's commitment to a professional library service, but he also believed that Milam had a "tendency to press the librarian-expert appointment in stations and in the Fleet more than necessary."[24] This reservation reflected a lingering doubt that perhaps trained librarians were not so essential. In a few years, the military's fragile commitment to quality library service became readily apparent.

Formal transfer of the camp library system to the military departments took place on November 1, 1919. Luther L. Dickerson was appointed library specialist in charge of army libraries and Charles H. Brown became the library specialist for the navy. All military points within the United States were covered by the transfer agreements. Remnants of the Library War Service outside of the country were turned over to the army and navy in June 1921. At the time of the initial transfer, the Association relinquished twenty-five camp library buildings, 921,293 books, and 164 library personnel. About 80 percent of the books went to the army. To ease the transition, the Executive Board voted to give $69,000 to the navy and $36,970 to the army.[25]

The Association worked very hard to effect a smooth transition; and the military departments gave every indication that their newly adopted library programs would be professionally administered and properly funded. Commander Mayo of the navy's Morale Division was enthusiastic: "I do not believe there will ever arrive such an opportunity as this to put welfare on its feet as a permanent adjunct to the Navy."[26] The army issued an official circular over the Chief of Staff's signature which committed that department to the "wise administration" of its libraries.[27] For several years, library service in the military departments appeared to be on a steady course; but the initial commitment to a professional library program declined perceptibly during the 1920s.

Although army libraries invariably enjoyed top-level endorsement, post commanders exercised considerable authority over the library program in their units. Unfortunately, many of these officers viewed the library as an extraneous activity. Corps area librarians, who maintained regional collections and travelled extensively to promote and to evaluate library service in the posts, became less effective as their travel budgets were reduced. When Dickerson resigned in 1924, he was not replaced. Between 1921 and 1931, appropriations for the army's library service plummeted 50 percent. The autonomy of post commanders and the permissive nature of library regulations were contributory causes of the decline. Overriding these factors was the army's miscalculation that effective library service could be rendered without trained librarians.[28] The navy's experience was similar. After Brown's departure in 1922, he was replaced by his capable assistant and former colleague at the Brooklyn dispatch office, Isabel Du Bois. Despite these reversals, library sections were not eliminated in either of the military departments. And when the next war broke out, there would be library programs to revitalize.[29]

The transfer of hospital libraries to the federal government was a prolonged and frustrating experience. Library service to U.S. Public Health Service libraries was an expensive item in the Library War Service budget. The Association did not want to discontinue the hospital library service without a suitable sponsor, but could not continue the annual expenditure of $86,000 for salaries and materials much beyond 1920. The Committee on the Transfer of Library War Service Activities was determined to find a way to preserve hospital libraries.[30]

On October 4, 1920, Herman H. B. Meyer of the transfer committee notified Dr. Hugh S. Cumming, surgeon general of the U.S. Public Health Service, that the Association would discontinue its service to hospital libraries in November due to "critically exhausted" funds. From the beginning, said Meyer, the Association had viewed the hospital work as a "demonstration service" which would eventually be taken over by the government. That time had now arrived, and the ALA was prepared to transfer all personnel and materials as soon as the Public Health Service would accept the responsibility. If the transfer could not be arranged, library work in the hospitals would be terminated.[31] Cumming expressed regret over the ALA's financial straits and believed that an equitable transfer could be realized within three months. Still optimistic several weeks later, Dr. Cumming told Caroline Webster that he was busy looking for the legal authority to assume the library service.[32]

Caroline Webster, who had guided the ALA hospital service since 1918, was professionally and emotionally committed to its survival. Webster took issue with what she thought was Meyer's perfunctory communication to the surgeon general. To the contrary, she believed, ". . . the work we have done puts us in a position to make certain demands."[33] Shortly thereafter, Webster submitted an advisory memorandum to Assistant Surgeon General Claude H. Lavinder which embodied those "certain demands." Assuming that the ALA's hospital library service would be transferred to the Public Health Service, Webster recommended a program similar to the one conducted for the past two years. Professional librarians should be appointed at every level to include the chief librarian, field supervisors, and hospital librarian.[34]

Milam and Meyer, perhaps more realistic than Webster, predicted a fiscal squeeze; and it soon materialized. Periodical subscriptions for the hospital libraries had already been cancelled in July 1920. Six months later, the Association was unable to pay the salaries of hospital librarians. Webster appealed to Ruth Emerson of the Red Cross' Bureau of Medical Social Service, who replied: "This is one of the most important parts of the medical social service; it must be continued."[35]

Upon Emerson's recommendation, the Red Cross approved a short-term loan to the ALA.

Despite this support, uncertainty over the fate of the program remained. The Public Health Service, eager to assimilate the ALA's library service, lacked the legal authority and funds to employ hospital librarians. In March 1920, Congress approved $100,000 for books in the Sundry Civil Bill, but made no apparent provision for salaries. Finally, on May 31, the Comptroller of the Treasury issued an opinion that personnel services were implied in the appropriation for books. The last obstacle was removed and the transfer to the Public Health Service occurred on July 1, 1921. Caroline Webster was selected to administer the new library section.[36]

Since the Public Health Service already had a director of library service responsible for the medical libraries, officials deemed it inadvisable to create a new position for the general hospital libraries. As a result, the Public Health Service would not pay Webster's salary. The embarrassing compromise was to designate Webster a consultant paid by the ALA who reported to the agency's director of library service. Almost orphaned in the first weeks of the transfer, the hospital library section struggled to furnish adequate service. Toward the end of 1921, a delay in the availability of government funds necessitated additional outlays by the ALA for library materials in the hospitals.[37]

By Executive Order of May 1, 1922, the administration of veteran's hospitals passed from the U.S. Public Health Service to the newly created U.S. Veteran's Bureau. Webster was designated chief of the Library Sub-section within the Medical Division, and continued on the Association's payroll. Supervision of the medical libraries was also entrusted to Webster's staff.[38]

Certain officials in the Veteran's Bureau held library work in low esteem. They viewed Webster and her staff as owing their primary allegiance to an outside professional group. Petty bureaucratic harassments were routine. Book orders were delayed and a clandestine investigation of the library program was initiated without the approval of the medical director. The report cast aspersions on the library service, questioned the competence of some librarians, and recommended that Webster be given the choice of resigning or accepting a $2,400 salary under the bureau. Fearing that the hospital library service was in great danger, Webster appealed to the ALA, prominent librarians, and other sympathetic organizations. Sensitive to the ensuing pressure from external sources, the bureau disavowed the report and vindicated Webster.[39]

Notwithstanding this outcry of concern for the welfare of the hospital service, Webster was not offered a permanent position by the bureau. She resigned on February 1, 1923, and was succeeded by Ola M. Wyeth, who in turn, was dismissed without warning on October 1, 1923. Abrupt as the break was, the interminable transfer was over. Relieved that the long ordeal had ended, Herman H. B. Meyer told the Executive Board that the connection with the bureau had ceased, "much to [my] satisfaction." It was, Meyer revealed, "a contact that was always disagreeable to me, unsatisfactory in its results, and very little accomplished."[40] The relationship was indeed uncomfortable and expensive for the Association. Subjected to niggling restrictions and disparagement, Webster and Wyeth endured the situation as long as they could, refusing to compromise their personal integrity or professionalism. Fortunately, the new chief of the library unit, Elizabeth Pomeroy, was able to strengthen the librarians' position within the bureau and to expand services.

No account of the Library War Service episode would be complete without at least brief mention of the ALA's postwar project known as the Enlarged Program. This project was a direct outgrowth of the wartime services and closely paralleled the nation's sense of buoyant expectation just after the Armistice.[41]

By war's end, the ALA savored the recognition which it had sought. Now ready to shed its prewar image of ineffectual leadership, the Association launched a reconstruction project—the Enlarged Program—fully expecting to establish the ALA as the dominant national force in library affairs. The Program began in early 1919 as a modest proposal to survey library services and professional education. By the time of the Asbury Park conference, however, momentum was building for a more ambitious plan and another major fund drive. Three areas were singled out for special consideration: continuation of war-related activities; constitutional revision; and new programs, which included increased expenditures for publicity, promotion of higher salaries for librarians, initiation of special services to immigrants, and creation of a National Examining Board to set standards for library schools. The ALA Executive Board authorized a $2 million fund drive and recruited a large staff, located in New York City. Carl Milam became director of the Enlarged Program in September 1919.

But divisive bickering among the membership, sporadic at first, built to a crescendo by early 1920. Some members feared a strong Association, others believed ALA headquarters would eventually move from Chicago to New York City, and still others did not want the ALA to continue supporting federal programs. These reservations, coupled with the public's weariness of fund drives, proved fatal. The ALA terminated the Enlarged Program in November 1920, unwilling to prolong the humiliation.

Shortly after the collapse of the Enlarged Program, the Association was asked to perform a task which symbolically closed the wartime venture. The Emergency Fleet Corporation, which mass-produced hundreds of freighters at Hog Island, Pennsylvania, between 1916 and 1921 to rebuild the nation's merchant fleet, invited many of the organizations which contributed to the war effort to submit names for the cargo ships. Milam polled the membership, which came up with such imaginative suggestions as ALABOOK, USALA, and THE OPEN BOOK. The final choice was uninspired: S.S. *ALA*. Christened by Shirley Putnam on December 18, 1920, the 9,000-ton vessel was renamed the ''Black Condor'' in 1935 and sold to the British in 1941.[42]

SIX

Reflections

World War I, however briefly, transformed the ALA from a small, aspiring professional body into a welfare organization serving the library needs of several million soldiers. The wartime experience, in turn, stimulated the Association to launch the stillborn Enlarged Program, led to the transfer of library services to the federal government, and influenced library development well into the 1920s. The Library War Service was indeed unique; neither before nor since has the ALA furnished direct library service to the military.

The selection of Herbert Putnam to supervise the Library War Service was crucial to the program's achievements. Putnam, the pivotal figure, drew upon nearly twenty years' administrative experience as Librarian of Congress. His own executive ability, coupled with his choice of talented assistants, contributed significantly to the administrative efficiency of the Library War Service. Soon after his appointment as general director, the Library War Service coalesced into a powerful, centralized bureaucracy. The centralization of authority in Washington was a new experience for the nation's librarians.

Bureaucratic organizations tend to standardize services and products. In the case of the Library War Service, there were three prominent examples of standardization: the camp library buildings; the technical routines of the camp libraries; and the overseas shipping cases. The erection of central libraries in the military posts was essential; without these facilities, all of the Association's books would have been distributed by other agencies. With only slight variations, camp libraries were built from a master blueprint, and this decision permitted the construction of the libraries within four months. Technical operations in the camp libraries, those functions related to the preparation of books, shelving, and catalogs, were relatively uniform and simple. The systemization of these technical operations enabled the camp libraries to open in record time and to provide efficient service without loss of access or control. Less spectacular perhaps, but almost as important, was the special overseas shipping case. These self-service cases protected the books in transit and were used as portable libraries for soldiers in remote areas in Europe and in the United States.

Neither the existence of a bureaucratic organization nor the tendency to standardize should obscure two other characteristics of the Library War Service, the pragmatic disposition to experiment with new forms of service and the degree of voluntarism associated with the war work. The performance of the Library War Service as an organizational entity has been stressed in this account, but the support of the Association by the nation's libraries and the general public was a crucial ingredient. Volunteer mobilization and cooperation at the local level preempted the need for either sustained coercion by the Association or major intervention by the government.[1]

The Library War Service was not an autonomous enterprise. Cooperative relationships were established with the Commission on Training Camp Activities, the military departments, and other social service organizations. The military services were supportive throughout the war. Although some military commanders were dubious about the value of libraries in the beginning, their reserve invariably turned to admiration. By virtue of its size, the YMCA became an indispensable outlet for ALA materials, especially in Europe. Senior officials of the YMCA were generally cooperative, but there was occasional difficulty at the operational level. Neither welfare group was immune to the normal quotas of jealousy and opportunism. The ALA was a zealous guardian of its resources and became uncomfortable whenever its materials were deposited with other organizations. For its part, many of the YMCA educational secretaries were not accustomed to libraries or their administration. Further, the YMCA was criticized throughout the war for exhorbitant prices and other irregularities in its services; and in this besieged state perhaps became overly defensive toward other organizations.[2]

Publicity was a vital component of the financial campaigns, the book collection drives, and the library work in the domestic camps and in Europe. Library publicity, used sparingly before the war because of its tainted association with the business world, became a powerful medium for the Library War Service. When the ALA went before the public with two major campaigns—the first fund drive in September 1917 and the second book solicitation in March 1918—the effect of publicity on the outcome was decisive. There is no direct way of measuring the impact of the general publicity within the camps or the impact of the vocational publicity after the Armistice. Indirectly, the consistently heavy attendance in the camp libraries suggests that the publicity was effective. In Europe, the publicity accompanying the books-by-mail service was demonstrably effective. The impact of these publicity assaults on the public's image of the ALA and libraries in general is problematical. The war-related publicity, extensive as it was, apparently did not have the residual influence which the architects of the Enlarged Program had hoped.

Librarians who served the Association during the war naturally brought their professional convictions with them. As heirs to the ideas articulated by the great "men of '76"—Melvil Dewey, William F. Poole, Justin Winsor, among others—librarians inherited a paternalistic service ethic and a fervent commitment to the library as an educative force. Not intrinsically associated with librarianship, these attributes were also shared by many professional groups. By World War I, this tutelary, elitist conception of librarianship had moderated. Librarians had come to tenuous terms with mass culture (popular fiction was usually tolerated), and had become more concerned with library extension, service to children, and administrative efficiency.[3]

Several significant, and sometimes antithetical, themes in the development of the American public library —elitism/paternalism, the library as an educative agency, mass culture, and bureaucratization—continued into this period.[4] These trends, all present during the war, coexisted peaceably. The emergency nature of the war work, the patriotic fervor of the times, and the unprecedented opportunity for librarians to display their professionalism no doubt contributed to this state of accommodation. Bureaucratization and calculated efficiency were enabling processes which facilitated the supply of materials and the provision of services. The bureaucratic nature of the Library War Service did not impair the development of a flexible, client-centered program. Librarians' elitism, though undeniably present, was more of a defense mechanism which enhanced their self-esteem than a harshly imposed concept of service. Lastly, the soldiers' educational requirements, as well as their recreational needs (mass culture) were each served without excessive prejudice.

During the war, librarians reaffirmed their belief in the book as a powerful determinant of human intellect and behavior. This faith in the power of print was pervasive: reading produced a contented, efficient army; reading advanced the cause of better citizenship; and reading hastened medical recuperation. Exemplifying this faith, William F. Seward, librarian at Camp Bowie (Texas), confidently proclaimed that "you cannot beat a reading army."[5] Betraying their elitist inclinations, librarians delighted in reporting the cultural works read by soldiers. After the war, libraries were heralded as stabilizing agents in the crusade against radicalism. By condoning the army's censorship of camp library collections, librarians conducted themselves in a manner which they judged was entirely consistent with the belief that reading had a profound influence. The inconsistency of this position would not be confronted for several decades.

Notwithstanding these vestigial attitudes, librarians performed exceptionally well under sometimes exhausting, stressful conditions. Unfamiliar with military customs and without permanent quarters, the first group of camp library organizers impressed the military authorities and the common soldier with their determination to provide a professional service. Never before had librarians been asked to serve such a cross section of the adult population. Having a captive audience (in the camps at least) of grateful soldiers undoubtedly inspired the librarians to extend themselves. Various services and programs, together with such features as accessible collections, testify to the emergence of a more pragmatic, liberal conception of librarianship. Permeating all of these services was the emphasis placed on library extension, the practice of dispersing library collections to as many locations as possible.

The Library War Service was not without imperfections. Competent librarians, especially in Europe, were always in short supply. The excessive loss of books between America and Europe severely reduced the effectiveness of library service in France. Seven million books for 4.5 million soldiers, as John Cotton Dana had bluntly noted, were simply inadequate. In spite of the Association's best efforts, many soldiers never got close to an ALA book. Certainly, female librarians did not receive an equitable share of the administrative positions in the camps, and the Association sometimes experienced an estranged relationship with the YMCA.

The Library War Service episode had immediate and long-term consequences. As the greatest mass demonstration of military library service in history, the Library War Service program was particularly successful in the short term. Librarians were proud of their contribution to the war effort, soldiers appreciated library facilities away from home, and military departments assimilated the ALA programs following the Armistice. Similarly, the hospital library service continued, first under the U.S. Public Health Service and then under the sponsorship of the Veteran's Bureau. Creation of the American Merchant Marine Library Association and the American Library in Paris were permanent legacies. The successful financial campaigns and the widespread approbation of its wartime services were heady experiences for an obscure professional association. Determined to build upon that record, influential members of the ALA devised the Enlarged Program to provide continuing support for selected war-related programs and to assume unprecedented responsibility for new services. Plainly unwilling to endorse a plan which would have vastly expanded the ALA's influence and services, the membership let it die.

In three areas, the Library War Service had a more subtle, long-term influence on the Association and librarianship: the commitment to international library development; support for an expanded federal role in relation to libraries; and adult education. The European phase of the war work and the importation problems experienced throughout the war highlighted the interdependence of the world's libraries. The destruction of great libraries during the war evoked tremendous sympathy from American librarians. After the war, the Committee on International Relations, which had been established in 1906, continued under Putnam's chairmanship as the general policy-setting group within the Association. New committees were formed shortly after the war to deal with specific requests for financial aid and other forms of assistance. For many years after the war, Putnam and other librarians were very active in the fund drive to rebuild the University of Louvain Library in Belgium.[6] And William W. Bishop, one of the ALA's wartime presidents, became the great internationalist among librarians over the next three decades.

For nearly three years the ALA worked closely with the military departments and other federal agencies. This relationship, together with a greater awareness of the nation's library inadequacies, contributed to the Association's postwar advocacy of greater federal responsibility for education and libraries. Confirming this new role, the Association endorsed two congressional bills in 1919.

The first, the Smith-Towner bill, introduced in July, called for the creation of a separate department of education within the federal government and recommended $100 million to be apportioned among the states for special programs dealing with illiteracy, Americanization, physical training, and teacher education. Section 10 of the bill stipulated that $50 million be spent to ''equalize educational opportunities,'' including ''the extension and adaptation of public libraries for educational purposes.''[7] This provision was historic; it was the first time that public libraries had been recognized as worthy recipients of federal funds. George F. Bowerman personally conveyed the ALA's unqualified endosement at a committee hearing. But the bill, despite its many supporters, offended states' rights and business groups. It failed to pass in 1919 and failed again after reintroduction in 1921.[8]

Another library-related bill, much more modest in conception, grew out of Edith Guerrier's wartime service with the U.S. Food Administration. The bill proposed a Division of Library Service within the Bureau of Education which would act as a clearinghouse for information concerning federal documents and their distribution to the nation's libraries. Although only $8,100 was requested to administer the division, the bill failed to pass. Guerrier pursued her goal until 1924 when the bill was reintroduced, and again met the same fate.[9] These early flirtations with federal library legislation served to convince the Association that it could not unilaterally mobilize the resources needed for national library development. In the years ahead, alliances with organizations sympathetic to library needs and a greater acceptance of a major federal role in library development became cornerstones of the ALA's national program.

The great interest in library adult education during the 1920s resulted from the convergence of many trends, some of which predated the war. Among these antecedents were individual reader guidance, use of community analysis as a tool to design services, support for special groups, subject departmentalization in large libraries, and library extension. Postwar developments contributing to the redefinition of the library's role in adult education included the growth of labor unions, the enfranchisement of women, and the recognition of widespread illiteracy. Traditionally, the public library considered itself an agency of self-education for those motivated to use it. This basically reactive philosophy was challenged by a more activist commitment to adult education. In 1926 the ALA Commission on the Library and Adult Education recommended new programs of reader guidance and adult learning.[10]

The emphasis on personalized reader guidance during the war created a lasting impression on librarians and became an important element of the adult education movement. The Carnegie Corporation, which funded the ALA commission, appointed Frederick P. Keppel as its president in 1923. Keppel maintained a strong interest in the ALA throughout the war, and as president of a major foundation he was in a unique position to befriend libraries. Judson T. Jennings, Matthew S. Dudgeon, and Charles F. D. Belden were among the members of the ALA commission. The popular self-study courses known as ''Reading with a Purpose,'' which began appearing in 1925, were descendants of Wheeler's ''After War Reading Courses.'' The appearance of these publications signified accelerating professional confidence, but also served to reconfirm an essentially prescriptive approach to library service.

The American Library Association and many of the nation's librarians embraced the singular opportunity to serve military personnel during the Great War. Librarians, together with their emerging professional association, joined with the federal government to do what they had always done best: select, organize, and disseminate the printed word for education and entertainment. The Library War Service surpassed expectations and performed its mission with distinction. Recognition and accolades accrued to the ALA, and a new generation of library leaders gained invaluable experiences which enabled them to serve the public and the profession more effectively. New horizons of professionalism and service were the enduring legacies of the American Library Association's participation in World War I.

SEVEN

Epilogue

Beyond the enumeration of themes, services, and consequences, one must reaffirm the contributions of individual librarians. The subsequent careers of selected participants in the Library War Service are hereby acknowledged. Herbert Putnam continued as Librarian of Congress until 1939, concluding a brilliant forty-year career in that post. The ALA's executive secretary until 1948, Carl H. Milam deftly guided the Association during a period of dramatic growth. James I. Wyer retired from the directorship of the New York State Library in 1938 after thirty years of distinguished service. At the age of seventy-five, Frank P. Hill retired from the Brooklyn Public Library in 1930 to become a consultant. McKendree L. Raney left the Johns Hopkins University Library in 1927 to become director of the University of Chicago Library, a position which he held until 1942.

Joseph L. Wheeler served as director of the Enoch Pratt Library, Baltimore, from 1926 to 1945, and became one of the profession's leading authorities on library administration and architecture. Married in 1923, Caroline Webster apparently never returned to the library profession. Beatrice Winser was appointed director of the Newark Free Public Library in 1929 and served in that position until her controversial retirement in 1942. Burton E. Stevenson remained at the Chillicothe Public Library, published many novels and reference works, and retired in 1957 after fifty-eight years in the same library. One month after Pearl Harbor he was busy preparing for another adventure, another global book crusade.

Major Army / Navy Camp Libraries (1917-1919)

Camp	Location	Librarians**
Beauregard*	Louisiana	George F. Strong Samuel A. McKillopp James R. Rutland William F. Yust
Bowie*	Texas	George F. Strong Irving R. Bundy Herbert E. Richie William F. Seward Grace D. Rose Lois W. Henderson
Cody*	New Mexico	Charles H. Smith Earl N. Manchester William H. Powers Clarence W. Sumner Edward Day
Custer*	Michigan	John S. Cleavinger Samuel H. Ranck Henry O. Severance Earl W. Browning

* Camp libraries constructed by the ALA.
** Librarians who served as permanent or acting camp library directors are listed in order of service at each location.

Devens*	Massachusetts	John A. Lowe Frank H. Whitmore James A. Lowell Ella R. McDowell
Dix*	New Jersey	Harold L. Hughes George H. Tripp Henry B. Van Hoesen James M. Johnston
Dodge*	Iowa	Forrest Spaulding Guy N. Power
Doniphan*	Oklahoma	Luther L. Dickerson William K. Porter
Fremont*	California	William E. Henry John S. Richards Sterling J. Talbot
Funston*	Kansas	Willis H. Kerr Purd B. Wright George W. Fuller Ferdinand Henke
Gordon*	Georgia	Albert R. Nichols D. Ashley Hooker Adam Strohm John W. Echols
Grant*	Illinois	James C. Barbee, Sr. Raymond L. Walkley Truman R. Temple Jesse Cunningham Joseph V. Cargill Earl N. Manchester Ellya C. Broomell
Greene*	North Carolina	Francis L. D. Goodrich J. R. Johnson William H. Duncan Winthrop H. Chenery William H. Blumenthal
Hampton Roads	Virginia	George H. Evans Louis W. Horne

Hancock*	Georgia	Robert P. Bliss
		Orlando C. Davis
Harrison, Benjamin	Indiana	William J. Hamilton
Humphreys	Virginia	Charles E. Rush
		William M. Hepburn
		Harold L. Wheeler
		William E. Langdon
Jackson*	South Carolina	Lloyd W. Josselyn
		Wharton Miller
		Orlando C. Davis
		John G. Moulton
		William S. Bangs
Jefferson Barracks	Missouri	Justus Rice
		(Mrs.) A. G. Coggins
		A. Earle Butler
Johnston*	Florida	Lloyd W. Josselyn
		Charles R. Green
Kearny*	California	Joseph H. Quire
		Mary L. Jones
		Lewis Galantière
Kelly Field*	Texas	Harold T. Dougherty
		Nathan R. Levin
		Edward Day
Knox	Kentucky	John B. Kaiser
		Max Meisel
Leavenworth	Kansas	Hattie Osburn
Lee*	Virginia	Henry S. Green
		Herbert E. Richie
Lewis*	Washington	Judson T. Jennings
		Edward E. Ruby
		Louis E. Castle
Logan*	Texas	Malcolm G. Wyer
		W. R. Watsabaugh
McArthur*	Texas	Willard P. Lewis
		Joy E. Morgan

McClellan*	Alabama	Carl H. Milam
		George L. Doty
		Ernest L. Johnson
Meade*	Maryland	Howard S. Leach
		Arthur L. Bailey
		George F. Bowerman
		Arthur R. Blessing
		Lewis H. Dielman
		Herman H. B. Meyer
		Charles M. Baker
Merritt*	New Jersey	Lewis B. Traver
		Carson Brevoort
		Harold F. Brigham
Mills*	New York	Charles H. Brown
		John E. Fitzpatrick
		Calvin W. Foss
		Arthur L. Bailey
		Eva R. Peck
Oglethorpe*	Georgia	Charles D. Johnston
		Raymond J. McCoy
Paris Island	South Carolina	Harold G. Russell
Pelham Bay	New York	Blanche Galloway
Pensacola	Florida	Charles A. Read
		Everett O. Fontaine
Perry (Great Lakes)*	Illinois	John F. Pelham
		H. Edward Roelke
		Matthew S. Dudgeon
		William D. Johnston
		Marcus Skarstedt
Pike*	Arkansas	Paul Blackwelder
		Winthrop H. Chenery
		Marcus Skarstedt
		George B. Manhart
		Reginald Brinsmead
Quantico	Virginia	R. W. McCulloch
Sevier*	South Carolina	Ralf P. Emerson
		Charles A. Read

Shelby*	Mississippi	Whitman Davis
		Glenn F. Davis
		Charles R. Bickham
Sheridan*	Alabama	Joseph L. Wheeler
		Louis J. Bailey
		F. D. Slocum
Sherman*	Ohio	Burton E. Stevenson
		Gordon W. Thayer
		George O. Ward
		Azariah S. Root
		Adolph E. Pauli
Taylor*	Kentucky	George T. Settle
Travis*	Texas	Joseph F. Marron
Upton*	New York	Galen W. Hill
		Frank L. Tolman
		George G. Champlin
Vancouver Barracks	Washington	Elizabeth J. Herrington
Wadsworth*	South Carolina	George G. Champlin
		Wiliam F. Yust
		John C. Sickley
		Francis K. W. Drury
		Earl G. Swem
		Weldom T. Myers
Wheeler*	Georgia	Frederick Goodell
		Adam Strohm

• Sources: "The Army's 'Index'," *Literary Digest* 58 (September 21, 1918):31; "Books Lauding Huns Barred Out of Army," *New York Tribune*, 26 September 1918, pp. 6-7; James R. Mock, *Censorship 1917* (New Jersey: Princeton University Press, 1941), pp. 153-71; and lists in RG 89/1/5 (8), American Library Association Archives, University of Illinois Library, Urbana, Illinois.

APPENDIX II

Books and Pamphlets Banned by the War Department *

America After the War, by an American Jurist. New York: Century Co., 1918.

Balch, Emily G. *Approaches to the Great Settlement.* New York: B. W. Huebsch, 1918.

Barbusse, Henri. *Under Fire; the Story of a Squad.* New York: E. P. Dutton, 1917.

Bennett, J. O'D., et al. *Germany's Just Cause: An Analysis of the Great Crisis by the Leading American Thinkers.* New York: The Fatherland Corporation, [1915].

Berkman, Alexander. *Prison Memoirs of an Anarchist.* New York: Mother Earth Publishing Association, 1912.

Bierce, Ambrose. *Can Such Things Be?* New York: Cassell Publishing Co., 1893.

——. *In the Midst of Life: Tales of Soldiers and Civilians.* New York: G. P. Putnam's Sons, 1898.

[Blackstone, William E.] *Jesus is Coming.* New York: Fleming H. Revell Co., [1918].

Boelcke, Herman, *Aviator's Field-Book.* New York: National Military Publishing Co., 1917.

Burgess, John W. *America's Relations to the Great War.* Chicago: A. C. McClurg & Co., 1916.

——. *The European War of 1914: Its Causes, Purposes, and Probable Results.* Chicago: A. C. McClurg & Co., 1915.

Carson, Capshaw, pseud. *A Witness Testifies.* Chicago: Carson Brothers Publishing Co., 1918.

Chesterton, Gilbert K. *Utopia of Usurers, and other Essays*. New York: Boni and Liveright, 1917.

Daniells, Arthur G. *The World in Perplexity*. New York: Review and Herald Publishing Association, 1918.

——. *The World War: Its Relation to the Eastern Question and Armageddon*. Washington, D.C.: Review and Herald Publishing Association, 1917.

Delaisi, Francis. *The Inevitable War*. Boston: Small, Maynard & Co., 1915.

Dernburg, Bernhard. *Germany and the War: Not a Defense but an Explanation*. New York: The Fatherland Corporation, [1915?].

——. *Searchlights on the War*. New York: The Fatherland Corporation, 1915.

Dewitz, Hrolf von. *War's New Weapons: An Expert Analysis in Plain Language of the Weapons and Methods Used in the Present Great War*. New York: Dodd, Mead and Co., 1915.

Doty, Madeleine Z. *Short Rations: An American Woman in Germany, 1915-1916*. New York: Century Co., 1917.

Eastman, Max. *Understanding Germany, The Only Way to End War, and other Essays*. New York: M. Kennerley, 1916.

Ewers, Hanns. *Let the Rulers Beware*. (Unverified).

——. *Vampire*. (Unverified).

Federn, Karl. *The Origin of the War: Facts and Documents*. New York: G. W. Dillingham Co., [1915].

Fox, Edward L. *Behind the Scenes in Warring Germany*. New York: McBride, Nast & Co., 1915.

Frantzius, Friedrich Wilhelm von. *The Book of Truth and Facts: Facts Which Every American Should Know*. Chicago: The Author, 1916.

——. *Germans as Exponents of Culture*. Chicago: n.p., 1914.

Free Speech and a Free Press. (Unverified).

Freytag-Loringhovern, Hugo Friedrich Philipp Johann. *Deductions from the World War*. New York: G. P. Putnam's Sons, 1918.

Frobenius, Herman. *German Empire's Hour of Destiny*. New York: McBride, Nast & Co., 1914.

Fullerton, George S. *Germany of To-Day*. Indianapolis: Bobbs-Merrill Co., [1915].

A German Deserter's War Experience. Translated by J. Koettgen. New York: B. W. Huebsch, 1917.

Glass, Kate Elizabeth (Perkins). *Her Invisible Spirit Mate: A Scientific Novel, and Psychological Lessons on How to Make the World more Beautiful*. [Los Angeles: McElheney, 1917].

Granger, Albert H. *England's World Empire: Some Reflections upon its Growth and Policy*. Chicago: Open Court Publishing Co., 1916.

Grasshoff, Richard. *Tragedy of Belgium: An Answer to Professor Waxweiler*. New York: G. W. Dillingham, 1915.

Harris, Frank. *England or Germany?* New York: Wilmarth Press, 1915.

Hedin, Sven A. *With the German Armies in the West*. New York: John Lane Co., 1915.

Henderson, Ernest F. *Germany's Fighting Machine: Her Army, Her Navy, Her Airships, and Why She Arrayed them Against the Allied Powers of Europe*. Indianapolis: Bobbs-Merrill Co., [1914].

Howe, Frederic C. *Why War?* New York: Scribner's Sons, 1916.

Hugins, Roland. *Germany Misjudged: An Appeal to International Good Will in the Interest of a Lasting Peace*. Chicago: Open Court Publishing Co., 1916.

Jeffries, Jouett. *War Diary of an American Woman in the Proclamation of the Holy War, 1914*. New York: The Fatherland Corporation, 1915.

Jones, Rufus M. *A More Excellent Way*. New York: Association Press, 1916.

Jordan, David Starr. *War and Waste: A Series of Discussions of War and War Accessories*. Garden City, N.Y.: Doubleday, Page & Co., 1914.

Kirby, William. *Manual of Camouflage, Concealment and Cover of Troops*. New York: E. N. Appleton, [1917].

———. *Manual of Gas in Attack and Defense*. New York: [1918?].

———. *Manual of Grenades and Bombing*. New York: E. N. Appleton, [1918?].

Labberton, John H. *Belgium and Germany: A Dutch View*. Chicago: Open Court Publishing Co., 1916.

Latzko, Adolph A. *Men in War*. New York: Boni and Liveright, 1918.

Leadbetter, Charles W. *The Other Side of Death, Scientifically Examined and Carefully Described*. Chicago: Theosophical Book Concern, 1903.

Leake, W. S. *How to Protect Our Soldiers*. (Unverified).

Lincoln, Ignatius T. T. *Revelations of an International Spy*. New York: R. M. McBride & Co., 1916.

McAuley, Mary E. *Germany in War Time: What an American Girl Saw and Heard*. Chicago: Open Court Publishing Co., 1917.

McCann, Richard M. *War Horror, Its Lesson to America: A Plain Statement of Facts, Not a Controversy*. New York: The Author, 1915.

McClellan, George B. *The Heel of War*. New York: G. W. Dillingham Co., [1916].

McGuire, James K. *The King, The Kaiser, and Irish Freedom*. New York: Devon-Adair Co., [1915].

———. *What Could Germany do for Ireland?* New York: Wolfe Tone Co., 1916.

Mach, Edmund R. *Germany's Point of View*. Chicago: A. C. McClurg, 1915.

———. *What Germany Wants*. Boston: Little, Brown and Co., 1914.

McManus, Seumas. *Ireland's Case*. New York: Irish Publishing Co., 1917.

Miller, Kelly. *The Disgrace of Democracy: Open Letter to President Woodrow Wilson* [Washington, D.C., 1917].

Mott, Lawrence. *The Searchlight*. (Unverified).

Mücke, Hellmuth von. *The 'Emden'*. Translated by Helen S. White. Boston: Ritter & Co., [1917].

Münsterberg, Hugo. *The War and America*. New York: D. Appleton and Co., 1914.

Nearing, Scott. *Open Letter to Profiteers: An Arraignment of Big Business in its Relation to World War*. [New York: People's Council of America, 1917].

O'Brien, Nora (Connolly). *The Outlook for Religion*. New York: Funk & Wagnalls Co., 1917.

Reventlow, Ernst von. *The Vampire of the Continent*. New York: Jackson Press, 1916.

Rohrbach, Paul. *German World Policies*. New York: Macmillan Co., 1915.

Russell, Bertrand R. *Justice in War-time*. Chicago: Open Court Publishing Co., 1916.

Schrader, Frederick F. *Handbook; Political, Statistical and Sociological, for German Americans and all other Americans who have not Forgotten the History and Traditions of their Country, and who Believe in the Principles of Washington, Jefferson, and Lincoln*. New York: privately printed, 1916.

Skinnider, Margaret. *Doing My Bit for Ireland*. New York: Century Co., 1917.

Souiny-Seydlitz, Leonie. *Russia of Yesterday and To-morrow*. New York: Century Co., 1917.

Thomas, Norman, ed. *The Conquest of War: Some Studies in a Search for a Christian Order*. New York: Fellowship Press, 1917.

Thompson, Robert J. *England and Germany in the War: Letters to the Department of State*. Boston: Chapple Publishing Co., [1915].

Trostsky, Leon. *The Bolsheviki and World Peace*. New York: Boni and Liveright, 1918.

Trotsky's Message. (Unverified).

Two Thousand Questions and Answers About the War: A Catechism of the Methods of Fighting, Travelling and Living; of the Armies, Navies and Air Fleets; or the Personalities, Politics and Geography of the Warring Countries. New York: Review of Reviews, 1918.

Viereck, George S. *Songs of Armageddon and other Poems*. New York: M. Kennerley, 1916.

Wilson, Theordora. *The Last Weapon, a Vision*. Philadelphia: John C. Winston Co., [1917].

World's Crisis in the Light of Prophecy. Washington, D.C.: Review and Herald Publishing Association, n.d.

A Brief Essay
on Sources

Sources for the study of the Library War Service may be classified into five major categories: contemporary literature consisting of articles, monographs, committee reports, conference proceedings, and public documents; reminiscences which appeared after the war; primary source materials; publications by historians of librarianship; and scholarly monographs and articles on the war and its aftermath.

Fortunately, many librarians published contemporary accounts of their wartime experiences. More often anecdotal than interpretive, these accounts appeared primarily in the *Bulletin of the American Library Association, Library Journal, Public Libraries,* and various state library association journals. The War Service Committee printed three annual reports (1918-1920) and issued two bulletins, the *War Library Bulletin* (1917-1919), and *War Libraries* (1918). These publications were particularly valuable for such subjects as finances, personnel, and book campaigns. Few librarians reflected on their World War I experiences in later years; important exceptions were found in the writings of Carl H. Milam, George B. Utley, Charles H. Compton, and YMCA librarian Ona M. Rounds. One contemporary monograph, Theodore Koch's *Books in the War* (Boston, 1919) is uncritical, episodic, and does not relate the ALA war effort to the broader context of American social history. Koch is still useful, however, for coverage of England's library program for military personnel prior to 1917, and for his analysis of soldiers' reading interests in the ALA camp libraries.

Without the vast amount of primary source material contained in the archives of the American Library Association at the University of Illinois, this study would not have been possible. The well-organized records of the War Service Committee are extensive (about fifty cubic feet). The collection includes personal correspondence, bulletins, policy manuals, newspaper clippings, personnel records, field reports, and photographs. Approximately 30,000 pages of correspondence and 10,000 newspaper and magazine clippings are preserved in these files. The correspondence of the coordinator of ALA's hospital library service, Caroline Webster, and the Executive Board minutes were also consulted. These contemporary documents supplement and verify the published record. Several topics, such as censorship, the ALA's relationship to the YMCA, and disagreements among Library War Service leaders are uniquely represented in the Association's archives.

Other relevant manuscript collections may be found in Washington, D.C. The papers of Herbert Putnam, divided between the Library of Congress' Central Services Division and Manuscript Division, provide insights into the formation of the War Service Committee and into Putnam's views on the suppression of books. The European dimension of the Library War Service is illuminated in the papers of Burton E. Stevenson, which are held by the Manuscript Division. Of special interest are field reports, library circulation records, American Expeditionary Force newspapers, and some exceptionally fine photographs. The National Archives hold three collections important to this topic. Records of the Commission on Training Camp Activities contain pertinent information on censorship and the transfer of the ALA libraries to the armed services. Records of the Bureau of Naval Personnel (Morale Division General Correspondence, 1918-1920) and the U.S. Army Adjutant General's Office Central Decimal Files (1917-1925) are helpful on the transfer of library programs to the government.

An unpublished report on the YMCA's overseas library work was obtained from the YMCA Historical Library in New York City.

No recent monograph or dissertation is devoted entirely to the ALA's World War I involvement, but several have shaped my views on certain events and individuals. Dennis Thomison, in *A History of the American Library Association 1876-1972* (Chicago, 1978), has summarized the World War I episode and devotes a chapter to the Enlarged Program. Thomison's study must be used with care; he relies too heavily on secondary sources. The early struggle (1876-1920) between library elitism and mass culture, a theme which reappeared in World War I, is explored in two provocative revisionist studies: Dee Garrison, *Apostles of Culture: The Public Librarian and American Society, 1876-1920* (New York, 1979); and Michael H. Harris, "The Role of the Public Library in American Life: A Speculative Essay" (University of Illinois Graduate School of Library Science *Occasional Papers*, No. 117, January 1975). Peggy Sullivan's *Carl H. Milam and the American Library Association* (New York, 1976) has contributed to my understanding of Milam's conception of librarianship and his administrative finesse. Claud G. Sparks has provided an exhaustive portrait of William Warner Bishop in "William Warner Bishop: A Biography" (Ph.D. dissertation, University of Michigan, 1967). This study clarified details of the feud between Herbert Putnam and Frank P. Hill.

Scholarly literature on the war is voluminous; therefore, only a few titles are cited here. Ronald Schaffer's *The U.S. in World War I: A Selected Bibliography* (Santa Barbara, 1978) is an excellent introduction to the literature. The outstanding administrative history of the war is Edward M. Coffman's *War to End All Wars* (New York, 1968). His extensive essay on sources is valuable for all facets of the war. Allen Churchill's *Over Here!* (New York, 1968) is a rather excitedly written account of homefront activities during the war. John M. Cooper, Jr. has compiled a selection of historical writings on the war in *Causes and Consequences of World War I* (New York, 1972). Historians represented in this anthology include Daniel M. Smith on American intervention and national interest, Arthur S. Link on progressivism, Allen F. Davis on welfare and reform, and James R. McGovern on prewar feminism.

Merle Curti's *The Growth of American Thought* (New York, 1964) is informative on social and intellectual trends during and after the war. David M. Kennedy incisively reviews the historiographical debate on progressivism in "Overview: The Progressive Era," *Historian* 37 (May 1975):453-68. Social services, including social work, are competently appraised by Clarke A. Chambers in *Seedtime of Reform* (Minneapolis, 1963). Jerry Israel's *Building the Organizational Society* (New York, 1972) contains some perceptive essays on twentieth century associational activities. John Higham's brilliant *Strangers in the Land,* 2d ed (New York, 1963) covers nativism and Americanization. Feminism during World War I is allotted a chapter in William L. O'Neill's *Everyone Was Brave* (New York, 1971). Repression of civil liberties is detailed by Horace Peterson and Gilbert Fite in *Opponents of War, 1917-1918* (Madison, 1957). Demobilization and postwar reconstruction activities are judiciously analyzed in Burl Noggle's *Into the Twenties* (Urbana, 1974).

References

Abbreviations:
ALA   American Library Association
ALAA   American Library Association Archives,
        University of Illinois Library,
        Urbana, Illinois
BALA   *Bulletin of the American Library Association*
LJ   *Library Journal*
LC   Library of Congress
NA   National Archives
WSC   War Service Committee

Chapter One: Organizing for Library War Service

1. Arthur S. Link and William B. Catton, *American Epoch: A History of the United States Since the 1890s,* 2d ed. (New York: Alfred A. Knopf, 1963), pp. 171-91.
2. N. Gordon Levin, Jr., *Woodrow Wilson and World Politics: America's Response to War and Revolution* (New York: Oxford University Press, 1968), pp. 13-28, 32-45.
3. Daniel M. Smith, "National Interest and American Intervention, 1917: An Historiographical Appraisal," *Journal of American History* 52 (June 1965):5-24; Charles V. Genthe, *American War Narratives, 1914-1917: A Study and Bibliography* (New York: David Lewis, 1969), pp. 1-22.
4. George Creel, *How We Advertised America: The First Telling of the Amazing Story of the Committee on Public Information that Carried the Gospel of Americanism to Every Corner of the Globe* (New York: Harper & Brothers, 1920), pp. 3-14, 455-59.
5. Link and Catton, *American Epoch,* pp. 208-09, 237-40; Horace C. Peterson and Gilbert C. Fite, *Opponents of War, 1917-1918* (Madison: University of Wisconsin Press, 1957), pp. 12-20; Frederick C. Luebke, *Bonds of Loyalty: German-Americans and World War I* (DeKalb, Ill.: Northern Illinois University Press, 1974), pp. 199-223.
6. Donald Johnson, "Wilson, Burleson, and Censorship in the First World War," *Journal of Southern History* 28 (February 1962):46-58; John Tebbel, *A History of Book Publishing in the United States,* vol. 2: *The Expansion of an Industry, 1865-1919* (New York: R. R. Bowker, 1975), pp. 88-89; Genthe, *American War Narratives,* p. 102. The National Security

League is examined in John C. Edwards, "America's Vigilantes and the Great War, 1916-1918" *Army Quarterly and Defense Journal* 106 (July 1976):277-76.

7. Arthur S. Link, "What Happened to the Progressive Movement in the 1920s?" *American Historical Review* 64(July 1959):833-51; Stanley Shapiro, "The Twilight of Reform: Advanced Progressives After the Armistice," *Historian* 33(May 1971):349-64; Clarke A. Chambers, *Seedtime of Reform: American Social Service and Social Action, 1918-1933* (Minneapolis: University of Minnesota Press, 1963), pp. 3-26; David M. Kennedy, "Overview: The Progressive Era," *Historian* 37(May 1975):453-68; Allen F. Davis, "Welfare, Reform, and World War I," *American Quarterly* 19(Fall 1967):516-33.

8. Robert H. Wiebe, *The Search for Order, 1877-1920* (New York: Hill and Wang, 1967), pp. 286-302; Samuel P. Hays, "Introduction—The New Organizational Society," in *Building the Organizational Society: Essays on Associational Activities in Modern America,* ed. Jerry Israel (New York: Free Press, 1972), pp. 1-15.

9. Mary E. Ahern, "The Librarians in European Distress," *Public Libraries* 19(October 1914):344-46.

10. [Editorial], *LJ* 39(September 1914):657.

11. [Edmund Lester Pearson], "The Librarian," *Boston Evening Transcript,* 16 October 1918, p. 7.

12. Ralph T. Esterquest, "War Attitudes and Activities of American Libraries, 1914-18," *Wilson Library Bulletin* 15(April 1941):621-23.

13. George Bowerman, "How Far Should the Library Aid the Peace Movement and Similar Propaganda?" *LJ* 40(July 1915):477-79. Bowerman's address to the ALA conference in Berkeley, California (1915) was not favorably received, as noted in "Libraries and the War," *Library Occurrent* 4(October 1917):229.

14. "The Library's Part in Solving this Problem," *New York Libraries* 6(May 1918):51-52.

15. Asa Wynkoop, "The Library and the War," *New York Libraries* 6(May 1918):59-60.

16. "Will the War Hinder Library Progress?" *New York Libraries* 6(February 1918):22-23.

17. Jessie Welles, "Unifying for War," *Wisconsin Library Bulletin* 14(February 1918):41.

18. "Is Your Library a Slacker?" *Wisconsin Library Buletin* 14(February 1918):39-40.

19. Edith Guerrier, *We Pledged Allegiance: A Librarian's Intimate Story of the United States Food Administration,* Hoover Library Miscellaneous Publication no. 1 (Stanford: Stanford Universtiy Press, 1941), pp. 10-43; Esterquest, "War Attitudes and Activities," pp. 624-28.

20. Ernest C. Richardson, "President's Address—The War Service of Libraries of Learning," *Papers and Proceedings of the American Library Institute, 1918* (Chicago, 1919), pp. 35-42.

21. "Vigilantes Object to Books in Newark Public Libraries," *LJ* 43(February 1918):117-18.

22. Esterquest, "War Attitudes and Activities," pp. 628-31. See also Peter Buitenhuis, "Writers at War: Propaganda and Fiction in the Great War," *University of Toronto Quarterly* 45(Summer 1976):277-94.

23. For the Lasswell list of propaganda titles, see Ralph T. Esterquest, "War Literature and Libraries: The Role of the American Library in Promoting Interest in and Support of the European War, 1914-1918" (Master's thesis, University of Illinois, 1940), pp. 191-95.

24. "Certain Enemy Publications May Now Be Imported by A.L.A.," *LJ* 43(August 1918):582-85; M. Llewellyn Raney, "The A.L.A.: Diplomat," *LJ* 44(September 1919):588-92; "Report of Committee on Importations," *BALA* 13(July 1919):330-38.

25. Peggy A. Sullivan, *Carl H. Milam and the American Library Association* (New York: H. W. Wilson Co., 1976), pp. 1-48.

26. Burton E. Stevenson, "Introduction [to Theodore Koch's *Les Livres à la Guerre*, 1920]," 10 June 1920, Burton E. Stevenson Papers, Box 24, Manuscript Division, LC.

27. Frederick P. Keppel, "Herbert Putnam," in *Essays Offered to Herbert Putnam by His Colleagues and Friends on His Thirtieth Anniversary as Librarian of Congress, 5 April 1929,* ed. by William W. Bishop and Andrew Keogh (New Haven: Yale University Press, 1929), pp. 255-56.

28. Walter L. Brown [President of the American Library Association] to Herbert Putnam, 30 April 1917, Herbert Putnam Papers, Central Services Division, LC.

29. James I. Wyer, "Library War Service," June 1917, WSC, RG 89/1/5(2); Tyler to Walter L. Brown, 21 April 1917, WSC, RG 89/1/5(1); Windsor to Walter L. Brown, 2 May 1917, WSC, RG 89/1/5(1), ALAA.

30. Putnam to George Reeder, 11 May 1917, WSC, RG 89/1/5(1), ALAA.

31. Putnam to Fosdick, 28 May 1917, WSC, RG 89/1/5(1), ALAA.

32. Fosdick to Putnam, 30 May 1917, WSC, RG 89/1/5(1), ALAA.

33. Putnam to Hill, 10 June 1917, WSC, RG 89/1/5(1), ALAA.

34. "Our Libraries and the War: Report of the Preliminary War Library Committee," *BALA* 11(July 1917):315-27. For the organization and composition of German travelling libraries, see "German Libraries in War Time," *LJ* 40(July 1915):482-83; J. H. Friedel, "The Travelling Library in the European War," *LJ* 41(September 1916):662-64; "Books for German Soldiers," *Literary Digest* 57(April 1918):31. Early work by state and local libraries is reported in Donald B. Gilchrist, "Libraries for the New Army," *LJ* 42(May 1917):347-49.

35. "Our Libraries and the War," pp. 315-16.

36. Ibid., pp. 320-21.

37. Theodore W. Koch, "Books in Camp, Trench and Hospital," *BALA* 11(July 1917):103-8. Koch extended his coverage of the British military library programs until the end of the war in *Books in the War: The Ro-*

mance of Library War Service (Boston: Houghton Mifflin Co., 1919), pp. 162-263.

38. William Orr, "Cooperation in War Work Between the Young Men's Christian Association and the American Library Association," *BALA* 11(July 1917):111-14.

39. Fosdick to Putnam, 28 June 1917, WSC, RG 89/1/5(1), ALAA.

40. Putnam to Fosdick, 27 June 1917, Herbert Putnam Papers, Central Services Division, LC.

41. Newton D. Baker, "Invisible Armor," *Playground* 11 (January 1918):479.

42. Raymond B. Fosdick, *Chronicle of a Generation: An Autobiography* (New York: Harper & Brothers, 1958), p. 147.

43. Fosdick, *Chronicle of a Generation,* pp. 148-50; Daniel R. Beaver, *Newton D. Baker and the American War Effort, 1917-1919* (Lincoln: University of Nebraska Press, 1966), p. 223.

44. Young Men's Christian Association, *Manual of Young Men's Christian Association Educational Work—Army and Navy* (New York: Young Men's Christian Association, 1918), pp. 3-15; Young Men's Christian Association, *Yearbook of the Young Men's Christian Associations of North America for the Year May 1, 1918 to April 30, 1919* (New York: Association Press, 1920), p. 133.

45. "War Camp Community Service—Its First Year," *Playground* 12(October 1918):273-322; War Camp Community Service, *War Camp Community Service and the Negro Soldier* [New York: War Camp Community Service, 1920], passim.

46. Fosdick, *Chronicle of a Generation,* p. 150.

47. Maurice F. Egan and John B. Kennedy, *The Knights of Columbus in Peace and War,* vol. 2 (New Haven: Knights of Columbus, 1920), pp. 62, 108-11.

48. Jewish Welfare Board, *The Jewish Welfare Board: Final Report of War Emergency Activities* (New York: Jewish Welfare Board, 1920), pp. 62, 108-11.

49. Evangeline Booth and Grace L. Hill, *The War Romance of the Salvation Army* (Philadelphia: J. P. Lippincott Co., 1919), pp. 352-56.

50. American Library Association, War Service Committee, *Report of the War Service Committee of the American Library Association for the Year Ending June 30, 1918* (Albany: ALA, 1918), pp. 7-8; American Library Association, War Service Committee, *Preliminary List of Books for Soldiers and Sailors Libraries* [Brooklyn: Brooklyn Eagle Press, 1917]; Matthew Dudgeon to Anna M. Price, 2 August 1917, Library—Dean's Office General Correspondence, RG 35/1/2, Box 22, University of Illinois Archives, Urbana, Illinois.

51. *War Service Library Week,* vol. 1, 15 July 1917. Copy in Library—Dean's Office General Correspondence, RG 35/1/2, Box 22, University of Illinois Archives.

52. "Resolutions Adopted by the Executive Board of the ALA, August 14, 1917," WSC, RG 89/1/5(1), ALAA; *Report of the War Service Committee, 1917-1918,* p. 31.

53. *Report of the War Service Committee, 1917-1918,* p. 4; Untitled report from ALA to War Department, February 1919, WSC, RG 89/1/52, Box I, ALAA.

54. Library of Congress, *Report of the Librarian of Congress for the Fiscal Year Ending June 30, 1918* (Washington, D.C.: Government Printing Office, 1918), pp. 9-10; Putnam to "Loyal Staff of the Library of Congress," 25 July 1918, Herbert Putnam Papers, Box 14, Manuscript Division, LC.

Chapter Two: Mobilizing Resources

1. Hill and Utley to [ALA members], 2 July 1917. Copy in Library—Dean's Office General Correspondence, RG 35/1/2, Box 22, University of Illinois Archives, Urbana, Illinois.

2. American Library Association, War Finance Committee, *Library Service for Soldiers and Sailors; the Story of the Million Dollar Campaign of the American Library Association* [Brooklyn: ALA, 1918], pp. 5-6.

3. Ibid., pp. 6, 10.

4. Ibid., p. 7.

5. Library War Council, *How to Conduct the Campaign for Libraries for Our Soldiers and Sailors* (Washington, D.C.: Library War Council, 1917). Copy in WSC, RG 89/1/5(1), ALAA.

6. Rossiter Johnson, letter to the editor, *New York Times,* 25 September 1917, p. 10.

7. Frank Hill and Morgan J. O'Brien, letters to the editor, *New York Times,* 26 September 1917, p. 12.

8. Rossiter Johnson, letter to the editor, *New York Times,* 1 October 1917, p. 12.

9. Marcus L. Hansen, *Welfare Campaigns in Iowa,* Chronicles of the World War Series, ed. by Benjamin F. Shambaugh (Iowa City: State Historical Society of Iowa, 1920), pp. 92-93; William H. Powers, "South Dakota's Contribution to Library War Service," *South Dakota Historical Collections* 10 (1920): 248-50.

10. *Library Service for Soldiers and Sailors,* pp. 7-8, 12-22; "High Goals Established by Numerous Cities," *War Library Bulletin,* 18 September 1917, p. 1.

11. "Banker Directs Choice of Books," *New York Times,* 9 September 1917, sec. 6, p. 9; Putnam to James Wyer, 1 December 1917, WSC, RG 89/1/5(2), ALAA.

12. Hill to Putnam, 3 December 1917, WSC, RG 89/1/5(2), ALAA.

13. Hill to Bishop, 16 July 1918, quoted in Claud G. Sparks, "William Warner Bishop: A Biography" (Ph.D. dissertation, University of Michigan, 1967), p. 221.

14. Bishop to Bulkey, 8 August 1918, WSC, RG 89/1/5(1); Bulkey to Bishop, 27 August 1918, WSC, RG 89/1/5(1), ALAA.

15. Wyer to Bishop, 17 October 1918, quoted in Sparks, "William Warner Bishop," p. 223.

16. American Library Association, War Service Committee, *Report of the War Service Committee of the American Library Association for the Year Ending June 30, 1918* (Albany: ALA, 1918), pp. 54-58; United War Work Campaign, *Report of the United War Work Campaign, Inc.* (New York: United War Work Campaign, 1921), pp. 7-13.

17. Frank P. Stockbridge, "Educational Programs of the ALA," *War Libraries*, 9 September 1918, p. 6; Stockbridge, "Newspaper Publicity," *War Libraries*, 10 October 1918, pp. 2-3. Many examples of the press coverage may be found in the massive clipping file (RG 89/1/18) in the ALA Archives.

18. Judson T. Jennings, "Three Reasons Why the American Library Association Needs Money for War Work," 1918, WSC, unprocessed item, ALAA.

19. "A Book in Camp is Worth Two on the Shelf," *Denver Times,* 6 November 1918, WSC Clipping File, RG 89/1/18, ALAA.

20. United War Work Campaign, *To Subscribers of the United War Work Campaign Conducted at the Request of President Wilson in November 1918* [New York: United War Work Campaign, 1919] pp. 16-17. Copy in WSC, unprocessed, ALAA; *Report of the United War Work Campaign,* p. 14.

21. Frank P. Hill to Carnegie Corporation, 7 July 1917, WSC, RG 89/1/5(6), ALAA.

22. Bertram to Wyer, 13 July 1917, Herbert Putnam Papers, Central Services Division, LC.

23. Wyer to Bertram, 14 July 1917, WSC, RG 89/1/5(16), ALAA.

24. Excerpt from Minutes, Carnegie Board of Trustees, 14 September 1917, in letter from Florence Anderson, Secretary of the Carnegie Corporation, to the author, 28 May 1975; Edwin H. Anderson to Putnam, 23 October 1917, WSC, RG 89/1/5(2); Putnam to James Bertram, 23 October 1917, WSC, RG 89/1/5(16), ALAA.

25. *Report of the War Service Committee, 1917-1918,* pp. 14-15.

26. "Report to Carnegie Corporation on construction and equipment of camp library buildings under a Grant voted Sept. 14, 1917," 1 October 1918, WSC, RG 89/1/5(16), ALAA.

27. "Books for the Camps," *War Library Bulletin,* August 1917, pp. 6-7.

28. George B. Utley, "The Library War Service and Its General Director," in *Essays Offered to Herbert Putnam by His Colleagues and Friends on His Thirtieth Anniversary as Librarian of Congress 5 April 1929,* ed. by William W. Bishop and Andrew Keogh (New Haven: Yale University Press, 1929), p. 487.

29. "War Service Work to Date," *War Library Bulletin,* January 1918, p. 1;

"The Great Gift of Books," *War Library Bulletin,* January 1918, p. 10; *War Library Bulletin,* February 1918, passim. For press releases, see WSC, RG 89/1/52, Box I, ALAA.

30. WSC Clipping File, RG 89/1/18; Pennsylvania Free Library Commission, "Suggestions to Pennsylvania Publicity Directors Named in Each Locality By Librarian to oversee Publicity Work," March 1918, WSC, RG 89/1/5(12), ALAA.

31. "How to Prepare the Books," *War Library Bulletin,* January 1918, p. 11; "Preparing Books for Camp Libraries," *War Library Bulletin,* April 1918, p. 11.

32. Brown to Dudgeon, 9 October 1917, WSC, RG 89/1/5(8), ALAA; American Library Association, War Service Committee, *Preliminary List of Books for Soldiers and Sailors Libraries* [Brooklyn: Brooklyn Eagle Press, 1917], passim.

33. Matthew S. Dudgeon to Charles H. Brown, 12 November 1917, WSC, RG 89/1/5(8), ALAA; *Report of the War Service Committee, 1917-1918,* p. 16.

34. Charles H. Compton, "What Then?" *LJ* 44(February 1919):100-101; American Library Association, War Service Committee, *Report of the War Service Committee of the American Library Association for the Year Ending June 30, 1919* (Albany: ALA, 1919), p. 21.

35. Dispatch offices were established at the following locations: Atlanta, Boston, Brooklyn, Charleston, Chicago, El Paso, Hoboken, Kansas City (Missouri), Newport News, New York City, Omaha, Philadelphia, St. Louis, San Antonio, San Francisco, and Seattle.

36. Untitled ledgers of overseas shipments from dispatch offices at Hoboken, New York, Philadelphia, Newport News, Brooklyn, and Boston, May 1918 to May 1919, WSC, RG 89/1/5(35), ALAA. For accounts of dispatch office operations, see Asa Don Dickinson, "Sending Books 'Over There'—The Day's Work in Hoboken," *LJ* 42(August 1918):573-74; and C. O. S. Mawson, "Uncle Sam: Librarian," *Bookman* 48(October 1918):220-27.

37. Hodgson to Carl H. Milam, 9 January 1918, WSC, RG 89/1/5(3), ALAA.

38. Mawson to McKendree L. Raney, 31 August 1918, WSC, RG 89/1/5(22), ALAA.

39. *Report of the War Service Committee, 1917-1918,* pp. 18-19.

40. Ibid., pp. 19-21; American Library Association, Library War Service, *Directory of Camps, Stations, Hospitals and Units Served and Librarians and Supervisors in Charge* [corrected to November 1918] (Washington, D.C.: ALA, 1918), pp. 3-4.

41. Richard H. Hall, "Professionalization and Bureaucratization," *American Sociological Review* 33(February 1968):94-95.

42. Personnel are listed in "Library War Service," *LJ* 42(November 1917):878-79; "Library War Service," *LJ* 42(December 1917):962.

43. Supplement to *War Library Bulletin,* June 1918. The figure of 1,100 to 1,200 library workers was extrapolated from the surviving Library War Service personnel records which are complete for surnames B-R. See WSC, RG 89/1/78, Boxes 1-2, ALAA.

44. Malcolm L. McBride to Putnam, 7 September 1918; Putnam to McBride, 9 September 1918, WSC, RG 89/1/5(39), ALAA.

45. Josselyn to Putnam, 13 September 1918, WSC, RG 89/1/5(39), ALAA.

46. McBride to Putnam, 23 September 1918, WSC, RG 89/1/5(39), ALAA.

47. Putnam to Priestley, 19 June 1918, WSC, unprocessed item, ALAA.

48. [Josephine Rathbone] to W. P. Dyke, 15 April 1918, WSC, unprocessed item, ALAA.

49. Female librarians comprised approximately 80 percent of the library profession between 1900 and 1920. Yet, women never held a majority of the leadership positions in national library associations, did not administer the largest libraries, and did not receive salaries comparable to those of male librarians. Female librarians fared better in most state and local associations, where they held a majority of the top positions. See Margaret A. Corwin, "An Investigation of Female Leadership in Regional, State, and Local Library Associations, 1876-1923," *Library Quarterly* 44(April 1974):133-34.

50. J. Stanley Lemons, *The Woman Citizen: Social Feminism in the 1920s* (Urbana: University of Illinois Press, 1973; Illini Books, 1975), pp. 3-40; William L. O'Neill, *Everyone Was Brave: A History of Feminism in America* (New York: Quadrangle Books, 1971), pp. 169-224. For an excellent pictorial review of women in World War I, see Nancy E. Malan, "How 'Ya Gonna Keep 'Em Down?: Women and World War I," *Prologue* 5(Winter 1973):208-39.

51. Winser to Newton D. Baker, 20 February 1918, WSC, RG 89/1/5(39), ALAA.

52. Putnam to Fosdick, 25 February 1918, WSC, RG 89/1/5(39), ALAA.

53. Putnam to Winser, 21 March 1918, Herbert Putnam Papers, Central Services Division, LC.

54. Askew to Milam, 6 March 1918, WSC, RG 89/1/5(5), ALAA.

55. Malcolm G. Wyer, [Report on Camp Logan], 20 March 1918, WSC, RG 89/1/5(16), ALAA.

56. American Library Association, *Papers and Proceedings of the Fortieth Annual Meeting of the American Library Association Held at Saratoga Springs, N.Y., July 1-6, 1918* (Chicago: ALA, 1918), pp. 283-84.

57. Ibid., pp. 286-87.

58. *Report of the War Service Committee, 1918-1919,* p. 28.

Chapter Three: 'Over Here': Domestic Service

1. [Matthew S. Dudgeon], "Instructions to Camp Librarians: Preliminary Draft," [November 20, 1917], WSC, RG 89/1/5(16), ALAA.

2. Ibid.
3. Edward R. Ellis, *Echoes of Distant Thunder: Life in the United States 1914-1918* (New York: Coward, McCann & Geoghegan, 1975), pp. 355-57. Although differentiated as camps and cantonments by military authorities, both types of installations were commonly referred to as camps.
4. Ibid.
5. Ibid., p. 362; Edward M. Coffman, *The War to End All Wars: The American Military Experience in World War I* (New York: Oxford University Press, 1968), pp. 59, 70.
6. Seward W. Livermore, *Politics is Adjourned: Woodrow Wilson and the War Congress, 1916-1918* (Middletown, Conn.: Wesleyan University Press, 1966), pp. 66-70, 73-78.
7. "Library War Service," *LJ* 42(December 1917):962-65.
8. Malcolm G. Wyer, [Report on Camp Logan], 20 March 1918, WSC, RG 89/1/5(16), ALAA; Paul M. Parham, "Malcolm Glenn Wyer, Western Librarian: A Study in Leadership and Innovation" (Ph.D. dissertation, University of Denver, 1964), pp. 112-14.
9. [Harold Braddock], "American Library Association," [November 1917], WSC, RG 89/1/5(16), ALAA.
10. Putnam to Raymond Fosdick, 20 November 1917, Commission on Training Camp Activities, RG 165, Box 412, NA.
11. James I. Wyer, "A Visit to the Camp Libraries," *New York Libraries* 6(May 1918):54-57; Wyer, "Report on Visits to Camp Libraries, March 7-25, 1918," 8 June 1918, WSC, RG 89/1/5(1), ALAA.
12. Hanmer to Putnam, 4 March 1918, WSC, RG 89/1/5(2), ALAA.
13. [Frank Hill], "Report to the Chairman of the War Service Committee of a visit to Certain Camp Libraries April 19-May 20, 1918," 8 June 1918, WSC, RG 89/1/5(1), ALAA.
14. See WSC, RG 89/1/5(5-7), ALAA.
15. Milam to Askew, 26 January 1918, WSC, RG 89/1/5(5), ALAA.
16. Askew to Milam, 28 January 1918, WSC, RG 89/1/5(5), ALAA.
17. American Library Association, War Service Committee, *Report of the War Service Committee for the Year Ending June 30, 1918* (Albany: ALA, 1918), p. 25.
18. Ibid., pp. 21, 26-27.
19. American Library Association, Library War Service, *Camp Library Handbook.* Washington, D.C.: ALA, 1918. Copy in WSC, RG 89/1/54, Box 1, ALAA.
20. *Report of the War Service Committee, 1917-1918,* p. 24.
21. *Camp Library Handbook,* pp. 22-27; American Library Association, War Service Committee, *Report of the War Service Committee of the American Library Association for the Year Ending June 30, 1919* (Albany: ALA, 1919), p. 45.
22. *Camp Library Handbook,* pp. 18-22; "Specifications for Uniforms for

Men," October 1918; Caroline Webster, "Uniforms for Women," 7 October 1918, WSC, RG 89/1/55, Box I, ALAA.

23. *Report of the War Service Committee 1917-1918,* p. 27; *Camp Library Handbook,* p. 30; "Library Service of the A.L.A.," WSC, RG 89/1/52, Box I, ALAA.

24. *Camp Library Handbook,* pp. 32-37; *Report of the War Service Committee, 1917-1918,* p. 18.

25. *Camp Library Handbook,* pp. 44-47; Joseph H. Quire, "Library War Service at Camp Kearny," *News Notes of California Libraries* 13(January 1918):26.

26. *Camp Library Handbook,* pp. 48-51.

27. Ibid., pp. 46-47; American Library Association, Library War Service, *Small Camp Library Handboook for Supervisors.* Washington, D.C.: ALA, 1918. Copy in WSC, RG 89/1/54, Box I, ALAA; A. M. Souby, "Cooperation between the various Y.M.C.A. Building Secretaries and the A.L.A.," 17 February 1919; YMCA Educational Survey Committee, "Standards for Camp Library Cooperation," [October 1918], WSC, RG 89/1/5(14), ALAA.

28. Theodore W. Koch, *War Service of the American Library Association,* 3d ed. (Washington, D.C.: ALA, 1918), p. 10.

29. American Library Association, Library War Service, *Soldiers, Sailors and Books* (Washington, D.C.: ALA, 1918), pp. 5, 16.

30. John Higham, *Strangers in the Land: Patterns of American Nativism, 1860-1925,* 2d ed. (New York: Atheneum, 1963), pp. 234-63.

31. Carol Aronovici, "Americanization: Its Meaning and Function," *Minnesota Library Notes and News* 5(December 1918): 181-82; John F. Carr, "The Library, The Friend of the Foreign Born," in U.S. Department of Interior, Bureau of Education, *Proceedings Americanization Conference* (Washington, D.C.: Government Printing Office, 1919), pp. 376-81; Jasmine Britton, "The Library's Share in Americanization," *LJ* 43(October 1918):723-27; George F. Worts, "What Books are Doing to Americanize Soldiers of Many Races," *Outlook* 120(October 1918):186-87.

32. Frank L. Tolman, "The Library's Aid to the Camp as a Melting Pot," *New York Libraries* 6(November 1918):126-27.

33. Theodore W. Koch, *Books in the War: The Romance of Library War Service* (Boston: Houghton Mifflin Co., 1919), p. 17.

34. "Publicity Helps," *War Library Bulletin,* February 1918, p. 8.

35. Frederick P. Keppel, *Some War-Time Lessons* (New York: Columbia University Press, 1920), p. 25.

36. "News from Camp Libraries—Some Informal Reports," *War Library Bulletin,* April 1918, p. 13.

37. Quire, "Library War Service at Camp Kearny," p. 21.

38. "Statistics of Camp Library Service—Main Camps Only," 27 June 1918, WSC, RG 89/1/5(18), ALAA.

39. W. Dawson Johnston, [Report on the Great Lakes Naval Training Station], [1919], WSC, unprocessed item, ALAA.
40. William F. Yust, "Rochester in the War Work of the American Library Association," in *World War Service Record of Rochester and Monroe County, New York*, vol. 3, ed. by Edward R. Foreman (Rochester, New York: Du Bois Press, 1930), pp. 201-2.
41. Ibid., pp. 199-201; "Not Enough Books for the Army," *Literary Digest* 59(October 19, 1918):26.
42. "News from Camp Libraries—Some Informal Reports," p. 12; Koch, *Books in the War*, p. 31; Ola M. Wyeth, "Camp Wadsworth Stories," *War Library Bulletin*, April 1918, p. 14.
43. Lewis Galantière, "Do Soldiers Read Trash?—No!" *Los Angeles Times*, 12 January 1919, WSC Clipping File, RG 89/1/18, ALAA.
44. "Bar Three State Library Books," Albany, New York *Knickerbocker-Press*, 18 February 1918, WSC Clipping File, RG 89/1/18, ALAA.
45. Putnam to Colonel R[alph] H. Van Deman, 23 February 1918, Herbert Putnam Papers, Central Services Division, LC.
46. Putnam to Tripp, 22 March 1918, Herbert Putnam Papers, Central Services Division, LC.
47. Koch, *War Service of the American Library Association*, pp. 19-20.
48. "Censorship Puts Grip on Camp Libraries," *Detroit News*, 31 March 1918, WSC Clipping File, RG 89/1/18, ALAA.
49. Colonel R[alph] H. Van Deman to Joseph L. Wheeler, 24 May 1918; McKendree L. Raney to Van Deman, 19 June 1918; Brigadier General M[arlborough] Churchill to Wheeler, 25 June 1918, WSC, RG 89/1/5(3), ALAA.
50. Captain G. B. Perkins to Commission on Training Camp Activities, 16 July 1918; Putnam to W. Prentice Sanger, 19 July 1918, Commission on Training Camp Activities, RG 165, Box 473, NA.
51. Library War Service to Camp Librarian, 31 July 1918, WSC, RG 89/1/5(8), ALAA.
52. "Books Lauding Huns Barred Out of Army," *New York Tribune*, 26 September 1918, pp. 6-7.
53. For a representative list of pro-German publications issued in the United States by various German propaganda agencies, see U.S. Congress, Senate, Committee on the Judiciary, *Brewing and Liquor Interest and German Propaganda, hearings before a subcommittee of the Committee on Judiciary on S.R. 307*, vol. 2, 65th Cong., 2d & 3d sess., 1919, pp. 1410-18.
54. James R. Mock, *Censorship 1917* (New Jersey: Princeton University Press, 1951), pp. 153-71.
55. [Edmund Lester Pearson], "The Librarian," *Boston Evening Transcript*, 4 September 1918, p. 7.
56. "The Army's 'Index'," *Literary Digest* 58(September 21, 1918):31.

57. "Books to be Barred from Library," *Library Occurrent* 5(October 1918):93-94.

58. Joan M. Jensen, *The Price of Vigilance* (Chicago: Rand McNally & Co., 1968), p. 148.

59. Mock, *Censorship 1917*, p. 170; George T. Blakey, *Historians on the Homefront: American Propagandists for the Great War* (Lexington: University Press of Kentucky, 1970), pp. 89-97.

60. "Secretary Baker Censors the Censor," *Publishers' Weekly* 96(November 1918):1722; Carl H. Milam to A.L.A. Representatives, 13 December 1918, WSC, RG 89/1/5(8), ALAA.

61. Blakey, *Historians on the Homefront,* pp. 82-159; Anna G. Hubbard to A.L.A. Representatives, 21 April 1919, WSC, RG 89/1/65, Box I, ALAA.

62. Burl Noggle, *Into the Twenties: The United States from Armistice to Normalcy* (Urbana: University of Illinois Press, 1974), pp. 13-16.

63. *Report of the War Service Committee, 1918-1919,* pp. 24-26. Herbert Putnam to the Camp Librarian, 26 November 1918, WSC, RG 89/1/55, Box I, ALAA. American Library Association, Library War Service, *Your Job Back Home: A Book for Men Leaving the Service.* Washington: [Judd & Detweiler], 1919.

64. *Report of the War Service Committee, 1918-1919,* p. 27; American Library Association, War Service Committee, *Report of the War Service Committee of the American Library Association for the Year Ending June 1, 1920* (Albany: ALA, 1920), pp. 40-42; Lloyd W. Josselyn to Malcolm G. Wyer, 25 February 1919, WSC, RG 89/1/5(12), ALAA.

65. Edith K. Jones, "The Growth of Hospital Libraries," *Modern Hospital* 18(May 1922):452-53; "Hospitals," *War Library Bulletin,* June 1918, p. 4; "Summary of Library War Service," *War Library Bulletin,* May 1919, p. 3; *Report of the War Service Committee, 1918-1919,* p. 17.

66. Caroline Webster, "Hospital Library Service: Its Organization," *LJ* 42(August 1918):563-64; Webster to Camp Librarians, 15 March 1918, WSC, RG 89/1/5(3), ALAA.

67. "Library Service of the A.L.A. in Hospitals," n.d.; "Hospital Library Circular No. 2," 1 July 1918, WSC, RG 89/1/52, Box I, ALAA.

68. C. H. Blair, "Relations with the American Library Association in Convalescent Houses," 20 June 1918, WSC, RG 89/1/5(13), ALAA; American Red Cross, *The Work of the American Red Cross During the War: A Statement of Finances and Accomplishments for the Period July 1, 1917 to February 28, 1919* (Washington, D.C.: American Red Cross, 1919), pp. 33-35.

69. Pomeroy to Webster, 12 May 1919; Strohm to Webster, 13 May 1919, WSC, RG 89/1/5(11), ALAA.

70. Caroline Webster, "A.L.A. Hospital Service," *LJ* 46(April 1920):305; "Hospital Library Circular No. 2," 1 July 1918.

71. U.S. Public Health Service Hospital No. 55, Fort Bayard, New Mexico,

"Annual Report of Library Services from June 1920 to May 31, 1921," WSC, RG 89/1/5(41), ALAA.

72. *Report of the War Service Committee, 1919-1920*, pp. 17-18.

73. Jones, "The Growth of Hospital Libraries," pp. 453-54. Other accounts by hospital librarians are Alice H. Rice, "Wanted—Books for Soldiers!" *Red Cross Magazine* 13(December 1918):27-32; Grace Schellenberger, "Library Service in a Reconstruction Hospital," *Iowa Library Quarterly* 8(April-June 1919):150-53; Mary Dale, "Notes from a Base Hospital Library," *News Notes of California Libraries* 14(January 1919):1-5.

74. Carl H. Milam, "What a Hospital Library May Accomplish," *Nation's Health* 3(November 1921):627-29.

75. Clarence W. Sumner, "A Hospital Library Service," *Hospital Service Quarterly* 2(August 1920):283-88.

Chapter Four: 'Over There': Service in Europe

1. Raney to Herbert Putnam, 11 February 1918, WSC, RG 89/1/5(33), ALAA.

2. Raney to Pershing, 20 February 1918, WSC, RG 89/1/5(14); Raney to Herbert Putnam 26 February 1918, WSC, RG 89/1/5(31); Pershing to [Raney], 22 February 1918, WSC, RG 89/1/5(14), ALAA.

3. Raney to Herbert Putnam, 26 February 1918, WSC, RG 89/1/5(31), ALAA.

4. Raney to Herbert Putnam, 10 May 1918, WSC, RG 89/1/5(31); Stevenson to Raney, 24 May 1918, WSC, RG 89/1/5(34), ALAA.

5. Stevenson to Morse, 20 May 1918, WSC, RG 89/1/5(34), ALAA.

6. Stevenson to Putnam, 21 May 1918, WSC, RG 89/1/5(34), ALAA.

7. Raney to Herbert Putnam, 10 May 1918, WSC, RG 89/1/5(31), ALAA.

8. Raney to Major G. L. Hamilton, 2 May 1918, WSC, RG 89/1/5(3), ALAA.

9. Stevenson to Herbert Putnam, 29 July 1918, WSC, RG 89/1/5(34); Stevenson to Herbert Putnam, 7 June 1918, WSC, RG 89/1/5(31), ALAA.

10. Stevenson to Herbert Putnam, 7 June 1918, WSC, RG 89/1/5(31); Frederick Goodell to Malcolm G. Wyer, 25 October 1918, WSC, RG 89/1/5(9), ALAA.

11. [James Hodgson], "Organization of the Sorting Station in the New York Public Library, Effective November 28th, 1917," December 1917, WSC, RG 89/1/5(3); Untitled monthly overseas shipping reports, WSC, RG 89/1/5(35), ALAA.

12. American Library Association, War Service Committee, *Report of the War Service Committee of the American Library Association for the Year Ending June 30, 1919* (Albany: ALA, 1919), pp. 34-35.

13. Raney to Burton E. Stevenson, 28 August 1918, WSC, RG 89/1/5(33), ALAA.

14. Putnam to Acting Quartermaster General, U.S. Army, 8 January 1918;
    Putnam to Richard E. Byrd, 5 January 1918, Herbert Putnam Papers,
    Central Services Division, LC; Frederick Pottle, *Stretchers: The Story of a
    Hospital Unit on the Western Front* (New Haven: Yale University Press,
    1929), p. 67; Raney to General Frank T. Hines, 24 June 1918; Hines to
    Raney, 9 July 1918, WSC, RG 89/1/5(3), ALAA.
15. R. L. Ewing, "Statement of the Work Organized in the United King-
    dom for the Men of the American Forces, May 1917-May 1919," 31 May
    1919, YMCA Historical Library, New York City.
16. William H. Taft, ed., *Service with Fighting Men: An Account of the
    Work of the Young Men's Christian Associations in the World War,*
    vol.2 (New York: Association Press, 1922), p. 506.
17. "Historical Sketch A.L.A. War Service from January 1, 1919 to Novem-
    ber 1, 1920," 1920, WSC, RG 89/1/52, Box I; "Overseas Personnel," 1
    May 1920, WSC, unprocessed item, ALAA.
18. Herbert Putnam to William L. Brown, 10 July 1919, Herbert Putnam Pa-
    pers, Manuscript Division, LC.
19. Burton E. Stevenson, "Report of the Operations of the Overseas Library
    War Service of the American Library Association to April 1, 1919,"
    1919, WSC, RG 89/1/5(34), ALAA.
20. Theodore Koch, *Books in the War: The Romance of Library War Service*
    (Boston: Houghton Mifflin Co., 1919), p. 91.
21. *Report of the War Service Committee, 1918-1919,* p. 34.
22. Stevenson, "Report of the Operations of the Overseas Library War Ser-
    vice."
23. Stevenson to Herbert Putnam, 12 June 1918, WSC, RG 89/1/5(34),
    ALAA.
24. Fosdick to Putnam, 1 August 1918, WSC, RG 89/1/5(3), ALAA.
25. [Edward C. Carter] to Burton E. Stevenson, 25 May 1918, WSC, RG
    89/1/5(14); Stevenson to Herbert Putnam, 8 July 1918, WSC, RG
    89/1/5(34), ALAA.
26. Stevenson to Putnam, 7 June 1918, WSC, RG 89/1/5(31), ALAA.
27. Burton E. Stevenson, "Some Reminiscences of the Paris Library," *LJ*
    69 (July 1944):574.
28. Elizabeth G. Potter, "Report of the Headquarters' Library, August 1,
    1918-June 1, 1919," 1919, WSC, RG 89/1/5(31), ALAA.
29. Stevenson to Herbert Putnam, 6 May 1919, WSC, RG 89/1/5(34),
    ALAA; Stevenson to Pershing, 30 May 1918, Burton E. Stevenson Pa-
    pers, Box 19, LC.
30. Potter, "Report of the Headquarters' Library."
31. [Burton E. Stevenson] to General Manager, Mail Transportation Dept.
    A.E.F., 12 August 1918, WSC, RG 89/1/5(34), ALAA.
32. Koch, *Books in the War,* p. 108; Untitled report on Paris Library mail
    department, Burton E. Stevenson Papers, Box 23, LC.
33. Koch, *Books in the War,* p. 109; "Historical Sketch A.L.A. War Ser-
    vice."

34. Mary E. Ahern, "Report on Publicity Work," [1919], WSC, RG 89/1/5(31), ALAA.

35. Samuel H. Ranck, "A Librarian's Job at Base Section No. 1," 12 May 1919, WSC, RG 89/1/5(31), ALAA.

36. Ibid.

37. Ibid.

38. Ibid. For another account by a white ALA librarian who served in a black YMCA hut at St. Nazaire, see Charles A. Read, "Library Experiences in a Camp for Colored Troops," *The Mess-KIT* (U.S. Army Base Hospital, Camp Merritt, New Jersey) 1(November 1919):18,23. Copy in WSC Clipping File, RG 89/1/18, ALAA.

39. Ona M. Rounds, *Buck Privates on Parnassus* (Boston: Meador Publishing Co., 1933), pp. 42-51.

40. Ibid., pp. 69,84-79. For another interesting account by Rounds, see *Rainbow's End* (Los Angeles: Overland-Outwest Publications, 1933), pp. 182-83.

41. Dixon Wecter, *When Johnny Comes Marching Home* (Boston: Houghton Mifflin Co., 1944), p. 273.

42. Anson Phelps Stokes, "Educational Memorandum No. 1: Plan for Work in American Army in France during the War," 13 February 1918; Stokes, "Educational Memorandum No. 2: Preliminary Plan for Work in American Army in France during the Period of Demobilization," 16 February 1918, WSC, RG 89/1/5(14), ALAA; Stokes, *Educational Plans for the American Army Abroad* (New York: Association Press, 1918), passim; Taft, ed., *Service With Fighting Men,* pp. 3-4.

43. Burton E. Stevenson to John Erskine, 17 September 1918, WSC, RG 89/1/5(8), ALAA; American Library Association, *A.L.A. Educational List: Books Furnished by the American Library Association for Use in Connection with Schools Established by the Army Education Commission.* Paris: ALA, 1919. Copy in WSC, RG 89/1/5(37), ALAA.

44. Willis H. Kerr, "Report of Educational Department," 30 June 1919, WSC, RG 89/1/5(31), ALAA.

45. Taft, ed., *Service With Fighting Men,* pp. 18-19; Luther L. Dickerson, [Report on the ALA Library at Beaune], 1919, WSC, RG 89/1/5(31), ALAA.

46. Dickerson, [Report on the ALA Library at Beaune]; American Library Association, War Service Committee, *Report of the War Service Committee of the American Library Association for the Year Ending June 1, 1920* (Albany: ALA, 1920), p. 22.

47. Dickerson, [Report on the ALA Library at Beaune]; Luther L. Dickerson to [John Erskine], [June 1919], WSC, RG 89/1/5(31), ALAA.

48. Quoted in Henry B. Van Hoesen, "Libraries in the Army Educational Program," *Education* 40(February 1920):348.

49. Dickerson, [Report on the ALA Library at Beaune].

50. Edward E. Ruby to Burton E. Stevenson, 1 June 1919, WSC, RG

89/1/5(36), ALAA; Katherine Mayo, *'That Damn Y'* (Boston: Houghton Mifflin Co., 1920), pp. 281-82.

51. Ruby to Burton E. Stevenson, 1 June 1919, WSC, RG 89/1/5(36), ALAA.
52. Ibid.
53. Ola M. Wyeth, "The A.L.A. Library in Coblenz," *LJ* 46(April 1921):351-53; H. H. B. Meyer, "Transfer of A.L.A War Activities," *LJ* 46(November 1921):938-39; U.S. Army, *American Representation in Occupied Germany, 1920-1921.* Compiled by Assistant Chief of Staff, G2. Vol. 2 [Coblenz: U.S. Army, 1922], pp. 286-88.
54. *Report of the War Service Committee, 1919-1920*, p. 14.
55. Ibid., pp. 14-15; "Report of the Temporary Committee, American Library Fund," 26 October 1919, WSC, RG 89/1/5(40), ALAA.
56. *Report of the War Service Committee, 1919-1920*, pp. 14-15; American Library in Paris, *The American Library in Paris, Inc.* Paris: American Library in Paris, [1921]. Copy in WSC, RG 89/1/5(40), ALAA.
57. James I. Wyer to Members of the War Service Committee, 9 January 1920, WSC, RG 89/1/5(40), ALAA; Burton E. Stevenson, "Some Reminescences of the Paris Library," pp. 575-77.
58. William N. C. Carlton, "The American Library in Paris, Inc." *LJ* 46(October 1921):831-34.
59. Susan O. Thompson, "The American Library in Paris: An International Development in the American Library Movement," *Library Quarterly* 34(April 1964):183; Minutes of the ALA Executive Board, 2 April 1921 and 27 December 1922, Executive Board and Executive Director, RG 2/1/1, Box I, ALAA.
60. Stevenson, "Some Reminiscences of the Paris Library," p. 577.

Chapter Five: Celebration, Decline, and Termination

1. Chalmers Hadley, "The Library War Service and Some Things It Has Taught," *BALA* 13(July 1919):106-11.
2. William W. Bishop, "The American Library Association at the Cross Roads," *LJ* 44(August 1919):489-95.
3. Herbert Putnam, "Statement of the General Director, A.L.A. War Service," *BALA* 13(July 1919):263.
4. John C. Dana, "Should Have Asked Millions More," in *The Use of Print*, vol. 1, no. 3, 25 June 1919, pp. 1,5. Copy in Burton E. Stevenson Papers, Box 25, LC. An earlier attack by Dana was published as "The Use of Print in Making War—and Peace," *LJ* 42(August 1918):579-81.
5. Copy of cartoon is located in WSC, RG 89/1/20, ALAA.
6. American Library Association, *Report of the War Service Committee of the American Library Association for the Year Ending June 30, 1919* (Albany: ALA, 1919), pp. 24-26; George B. Utley, memorandum to accompany publicity materials, 30 October 1919, WSC, RG 89/1/5(38), ALAA.

7. The three bibliographies were *Eight Hundred Useful Books,* compiled by Sophy H. Powell. [Washington, D.C: F. J. Haskin, 1920]; *Five Hundred Business Books,* compiled by Ethel Cleland. Washington, D.C.: ALA, 1919-1920; and *One Thousand Technical Books,* compiled by Herbert L. Cowing. Washington, D.C.: ALA, 1919.

8. American Library Association, Library War Service, *The Job Book for Men Leaving the Service.* Edited by Joseph L. Wheeler. Washington, D.C: ALA, 1919; American Library Association, Library War Service, *Books at Work in the War During the Armistice and After.* Washington, D.C.: ALA, 1919; Carl H. Milam, "Statement of the Acting General Director to the War Service Committee," 1 September 1919, WSC, RG 89/1/5(1), ALAA.

9. U.S. Department of Interior, Bureau of Education, *Report of the Commissioner of Education for the Year Ended June 30, 1927* (Washington, D.C.: Government Printing Office, 1927), p. 25; U.S. Department of Interior, Bureau of Education, *Report of the Commissioner of Education for the Year Ended June 30, 1928* (Washington, D.C.: Government Printing Office, 1928), p. 31.

10. *Report of the War Service Committee, 1918-19,* p. 24; "Report of Committee on Transfer of Library War Service Activities," *LJ* 45(November, 1920):942; American Library Association, War Service Committee, *Report of the War Service Committee of the American Library Association for the Year Ending June 1, 1920* (Albany: ALA, 1920), p. 8.

11. On ALA service to the navy, see Charles H. Brown, "Naval Libraries— Present and Future," *LJ* 44(April 1919):235-41; Theodore W. Koch, *Books in the War: The Romance of Library War Service* (Boston: Houghton Mifflin Co., 1919):123-43; "Historical Sketch A.L.A. War Service from January 1, 1919 to November 1, 1920," 1920, WSC, RG 89/1/52, Box I, ALAA.

12. Captain Ryland Drennan to all Masters of United States Shipping Board Vessels, 24 July 1919, WSC, RG 89/1/5(22); Forrest B. Spaulding to A.L.A. Dispatch Officers and Supervisors, 3 December 1919, WSC, RG 89/1/5(22); Carl H. Milam, "Secretary's Report [1920-21]," *BALA* 15(November 1921):4.

13. Elizabeth B. Tower, "The Story of the American Merchant Marine Library Association," *Special Libraries* 14(May 1923):69-72.

14. Aaron I. Michelson, "The American Merchant Marine Library Association: Its History and Functions" (Master's thesis, Western Reserve University, 1950), pp. 1-17.

15. Gertrude T. Rider to Carl H. Milam, 8 May 1920, WSC, RG 89/1/5(47), ALAA.

16. American Library Association, Library War Service, "Authors Provide Books for War-Blind," n.d., WSC, RG 89/1/5(44), ALAA.

17. Keller to J. R. Rutland, n.d., WSC RG 89/1/21, Box I, ALAA.

18. *Report of the War Service Committee, 1918-1919,* p. 75; Carl H. Milam,

untitled memorandum, 12 December 1919, WSC, RG 89/1/5, Box I, ALAA.

19. *Report of the War Service Committee, 1918-1919,* pp. 7,58-59.

20. *Report of the War Service Committee, 1918-1919,* p. 68; "American Library Association War Service Committee Minutes of January 29, 1919," WSC, RG 89/1/5(1), ALAA.

21. James I. Wyer to Major Jason S. Joy, 5 March 1919, WSC, RG 89/1/5(33), ALAA. Major Joy succeeded Fosdick as chairman of the Commission on Training Camp Activities.

22. Marion Jackson to James I. Wyer, 6 March 1919, WSC, RG 89/1/5(33), ALAA. Jackson was secretary of the Naval Commission on Training Camp Activities. The Naval Commission, created in 1917, was the navy's version of the original Army Commission. Fosdick directed both commissions during the war.

23. Milam to Major A. E. Foote, 25 July 1919, Commission on Training Camp Activities, RG 165, Box 557, NA.

24. Captain (chaplain) J. F. B. Carruthers, "Memorandum in re Interview with Carl H. Milam," Records of the Bureau of Naval Personnel, Morale Division General Correspondence (1918-1920), RG 24, Box 20, NA.

25. *Report of the War Service Committee, 1919-1920,* pp. 5,47; "Report on Army and Navy Points Filing Transfers and Inventories with A.L.A. War Service, Oct. 31, 1919," 25 February 1920, WSC, RG 89/1/52, Box I, ALAA.

26. Commander C[laude] B. Mayo to Chief, Bureau of Navigation, 4 November 1919, Records of the Bureau of Naval Personnel, Morale Division General Correspondence (1918-1920), RG 24, Box 20, NA.

27. U.S. War Department, Army Library Service. Circular No. 480, 21 October 1919. Copy in Adjutant General's Office Central Decimal Files (1917-1925), RG 407, Box 741, NA.

28. John Jamieson, *Books for the Army: The Army Library Service in the Second World War* (New York: Columbia University Press, 1950), pp. 16-19.

29. *U.S. Army, Annual Reports of the Navy Department for the Fiscal Year 1927* (Washington, D.C.: Government Printing Office, 1928), p. 177. For information about navy library services in the 1920s, see Ralph M. Dunbar, "Library Work Aboard Naval Vessels," *LJ* 48(December 1923):995-98; Isabel Du Bois, "Organization of Libraries of the U.S. Navy," *LJ* 49(June 1924):519-24: and Du Bois, "Value of Naval Hospital Libraries," *U.S. Naval Medical Bulletin* 23(November 1925):403-06.

30. Caroline Webster, "A.L.A. Hospital Service," *LJ* 46(April 1921):305; "Supplementary Report of the Committee on the Transfer of Library War Service," 18 December 1920, WSC, RG 89/1/5(43), ALAA.

31. Meyer to Cumming, 4 October 1920, WSC, RG 89/1/5(42), ALAA.

32. Cumming to Webster, 29 October 1920, WSC, RG 89/1/5(42), ALAA.

33. Webster to Carl H. Milam, 8 October 1920, WSC, RG 89/1/5(43), ALAA.

34. Caroline Webster, "Memorandum on Hospital Library Service Submitted at the Request of Assistant Surgeon General C. H. Lavinder," October 1920, WSC, RG 89/1/5(43), ALAA.

35. Webster, "A.L.A. Hospital Service," p. 306.

36.. Herman H. B. Meyer to Caroline Webster, 19 February 1921; Meyer to Webster, 21 March 1921, WSC, RG 89/1/5(43), ALAA; American Library Association, *Papers and Proceedings of the Forty-Third Annual Meeting of the American Library Association Held at Swampscott, Massachusetts, June 20-25, 1921* (Chicago: ALA, 1921), p. 98.

37. American Library Association, *Papers and Proceedings of the Forty-Fourth Annual Meeting of the American Library Association Held at Detroit, Michigan, June 26-July 1, 1922* (Cicago: ALA, 1922), pp. 219-20; Ola M. Wyeth, [Report on Hospital Library Service 1921-1923], 10 December 1923, WSC, RG 89/1/52, Box 52, ALAA. Wyeth was Webster's chief assistant from 1921 to February 1, 1923, when she became head of the library unit in the Veteran's Bureau. Wyeth's detailed, candid report was submitted to Carl H. Milam. It was never published.

38. Elizabeth Pomeroy, "U.S. Veterans' Hospital Library Service," *LJ* 50(March 1925):253-54.

39. Wyeth, [Report on Hospital Library Service 1921-1923].

40. Minutes of the Executive Board, 29 June 1924, Executive Board and Executive Director, RG 2/1/1, Box 2, ALAA.

41. For an extensive discussion of the Enlarged Program, consult Arthur P. Young, "The American Library Association and World War I" (Ph.D. dissertation, University of Illinois at Urbana-Champaign, 1976), pp. 226-59.

42. Milam to Members of the American Library Association, 28 April 1920, WSC, RG 89/1/5(39); "The Launching of the ALA," *LJ* 46(January 1921):25-26; "The Lady Was a Tramp Steamer: The Good Ship ALA," *American Libraries* 7(April 1976):194-95.

Chapter Six: Reflections

1. For a perceptive reassessment of voluntarism in World War I, see Robert D. Cuff, "Herbert Hoover, The Ideology of Voluntarism and War Organization During the Great War," *Journal of American History* 64(September 1977):358-72.

2. Owen E. Pence, *The Y.M.C.A. and Social Needs: A Study in Institutional Adaptation* (New York: Association Press, 1939), pp. 140-42.

3. Cf. Dee Garrison, *Apostles of Culture: The Public Librarian and American Society, 1876-1920* (New York: Free Press, 1979), passim.

4. Cf. Michael H. Harris, "The Role of the Public Library in American Life: A Speculative Essay," University of Illinois Graduate School of Library

Science *Occasional Papers,* No. 117, January 1975, passim.

5. William F. Seward, "Leaves from a Camp Librarian's Notebook," *Bookman* 48(November 1918):281.

6. "Drive for Louvain Library Fund," *LJ* 47(April 1922):309; "The Louvain Library," *BALA* 17(January 1923):32-33.

7. U.S. Congress, House, Committee on Education, Senate Committee on Education and Labor, *Education bill [to create a Department of Education], Joint Hearing before the Committees of Education and Labor on H.R. 7 and S. 1017.* 66th Cong., 1st sess., 1919, pp. 7-8; Joy E. Morgan, "An Opportunity for Librarians," *Public Libraries* 25(November 1920):546-47.

8. J. Stanley Lemons, *The Woman Citizen: Social Feminism in the 1920s* (Urbana: University of Illinois Press, 1973; Illini Books, 1975), pp. 128-29.

9. U.S. Congress, House, Committee on Education, *A Library Information Service, Hearing before the Committee on Education on H.R. 6870.* 66th Cong., 1st sess., 1919; U.S. Congress, House, Committee on Education, *Library Information Service, Hearing before the Committee on Education on H.R. 633.* 68th Cong., 1st sess., 1924.

10. Robert E. Lee, *Continuing Education for Adults Through the American Public Library 1833-1964* (Chicago: ALA, 1966), pp. 45-55; Margaret E. Monroe, *Library Adult Education: The Biography of an Idea* (New York: Scarecrow Press, 1963), pp. 20-34.

INDEX

145

Two thousand copies of *Books for Sammies* were printed by the University of Kentucky Printing Services. The text is set in Garamond type and printed on Mohawk Superfine 80-lb paper. Design specifications and invaluable aesthetic counsel were graciously provided by Mr. Glenn House, assistant professor in the Graduate School of Library Service, University of Alabama, and director of the Gorgas Oak Press.